STEP BY STEP THROUGH THE BIBLE

Puzzles, Quizzes, and Writing Experiences for Teaching Important Biblical Passages

Jean Louise Gustafson
and
Christine L. Poziemski

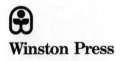

Winston Press

To our parents,
who encouraged us

Grateful acknowledgment is made to the following people for their help and encouragement: Mark Gustafson, Dusty Sang, Jerry Stroud and Mary Latondress Nosaka.

Illustrations by Joyce Markin
Cover design by Nancy Condon

ISBN: 0-86683-835-X
Printed in the United States of America
9 8 7 6 5 4 3 2 1
Winston Press
430 Oak Grove
Minneapolis, Minnesota 55403

Contents

Introduction

Step by Step Through the Bible is based on Bible highlights from the Old and New Testaments. The book was created for use with intermediate, junior, and senior high school students, and can be used in the classroom, or at home by individuals or families. It can be used as a basic overview of the Bible, or it can be used as a supplementary text. Most importantly, this book is designed to work well with any translation of the Bible.

Each activity encourages creativity. The students imagine that they are living in biblical times. They become playwrights and choose Noah and his family as the cast of characters. They interview Abraham's wife and son. They even illustrate stained glass windows depicting Jesus' entry into Jerusalem.

In addition to encouraging creativity, this book is designed to make the men and women of the Bible real to young people. In one activity the students choose pictures from a magazine to make an Israelite's scrapbook. In another they design a television series entitled "One Week in the Life of Samson."

Finally, *Step by Step Through the Bible* promotes Bible knowledge. There is more than one activity for each Bible passage as well as review activities at the end of each unit. "Who's Who" asks students to identify important people of the Bible, while puzzles, mazes and other games make review entertaining.

Students can use the book as individuals, or be divided into groups to work together on activities. The teacher may wish to assign specific activities to groups based on their artistic or literary abilities. Varying tastes of students may also influence the teacher's decision. The book can also be used with individuals for enrichment.

Directions for each activity are clearly stated. The Resources section functions as an answer key and provides background and information for the teacher. The Resources section also suggests discussion helps and optional methods for using the material.

The authors are experienced teachers who have used the activities in their own classrooms. Other teachers have found the activities in this book to be worthwhile and a welcome change of pace. Most of all, this book is designed to be fun. Have a good time with your students. Share the excitement of opening young minds to the Bible.

Beginnings

CREATION

Genesis 1:1—2:4a

Activity 1

Directions: Draw a symbol for each day of creation by using the numbers of the days as part of each symbol.

Example:

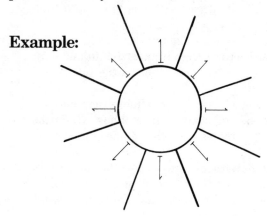

CREATION

Genesis 1:1—2:4a

Directions: Write two pattern poems by following the example below.

FORMULA

subject

two words that describe God

three words showing actions of God

phrase of four words about God

another word for God

POEM

God

powerful, wonderful

existing, molding, organizing

transformed the awesome void

creator

POEM #1

subject

two words that describe creation

three words showing actions
    attributed to creation

phrase of four words about
    creation

Creation _____

_____

_____

_____

_____

_____

POEM #2

subject

two words that describe God

three words showing actions
    attributed to God

phrase of four words about
    God

another word for God

God _____

_____

_____

_____

_____

_____

_____

CREATION OF MAN AND WOMAN

Activity 3

Genesis 2:4—2:25

Directions: First, list qualities of Eden. Then, write down similarities or differences between Eden and our society.

EDEN	OUR SOCIETY
1. IMMORTALITY	1. INEVITABLE DEATH
2.	2.
3.	3.
4.	4.
5.	5.
6.	6.
7.	7.
8.	8.
9.	9.
10.	10.

CREATION OF MAN AND WOMAN

Genesis 2:4—2:25

Directions: Imagine that you are Adam and you have just experienced your first day on earth—a walk around the Garden of Eden, the naming of creatures, and finally the surprise of a more suitable companion. As Adam, complete this diary entry.

Day 1

Dear Diary,

A Most Amazed Adam

ORIGIN OF SIN

Genesis 3:1-24

Directions: Label the apples on the tree below with evil that people would not know about if they had not disobeyed and eaten from the forbidden tree.

ORIGIN OF SIN

Genesis 3:1-24

Directions: Below are illustrations of scenes from the story in Genesis 3:1-24. Number the pictures chronologically and beneath each fill in the portion of the story that applies.

_____

_____

_____

_____

_____

_____

_____

_____

_____

_____

_____

_____

_____

_____

_____

_____

_____

_____

CAIN AND ABEL

Genesis 4:1-16

Directions: Respond to the following statements with *true, false,* or *not mentioned.*

_____ 1. Adam and Eve had one son older than Abel.

_____ 2. Before Cain killed Abel, God warned him that he would have to fight temptation.

_____ 3. Abel suggested that he and his brother go into the field to discuss God's rejection.

_____ 4. God placed a mark on Cain to ensure his separation from other people.

_____ 5. God rejected not only Cain's offering but also Cain.

_____ 6. God said that if anyone killed Cain, seven people would die to avenge his death.

_____ 7. The reason for God's rejection of Cain's offering was that Cain had not offered his best.

_____ 8. Cain's "mark" was placed on his forehead.

_____ 9. God said that he knew Abel was dead because his spirit cried out to him from the air.

_____ 10. Eve wept forty days and forty nights after Abel's death.

_____ 11. The curse placed on Cain was that he could no longer farm but would have to wander instead.

_____ 12. Cain expected that God would be more pleased with Abel's gift than with his own.

CAIN AND ABEL

Genesis 4:1-16

Directions: Make a coat of arms for Cain by drawing your responses to the questions below on the shield. Then write an appropriate saying or slogan on the banner below the shield.

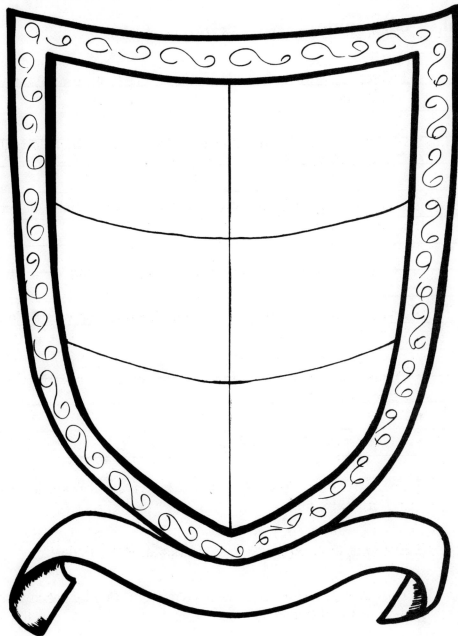

1. What was Cain's position in his family?
2. What was Cain's occupation?
3. What were Cain's feelings toward his brother?
4. What was Cain's sacrifice?
5. Draw a picture representing Cain's most dramatic action.
6. What was Cain's punishment?
7. Color half of the shield with a color that you think fits Cain's personality.

THE FLOOD

Genesis 6:9—9:17

Directions: Make a list of ten to fifteen words describing Noah. Use the endings suggested.

-ing,   -ful,   -ed,   -able,   -ly,   -est

1. _____
2. _____
3. _____
4. _____
5. _____
6. _____
7. _____
8. _____
9. _____
10. _____
11. _____
12. _____
13. _____
14. _____
15. _____

THE FLOOD

Genesis 6:9—9:17

Directions: Write the dialogue for a scene from the following play. Include the total cast of characters in the scene.

Noah on Dry Land

Setting: The day that Noah and his family embark on dry land in the Ararat mountain range. God has told them to leave the ark, and they are now standing on the mountain.

Characters: *Noah*—strong willed.

Noah's wife—soft spoken, easily influenced by Noah.

Shem—Noah's oldest son, handsome, Noah's favorite.

Ham—Noah's second son, a follower of his older brother.

Japheth—the youngest of Noah's sons, spoiled by his mother, a complainer.

TOWER OF BABEL

Activity 11

Genesis 11:1-9

Directions: Before reading the Scripture passage, list the first names of all class members on the lines provided. Using a book of name origins or an unabridged dictionary, explain what the names originally meant. Then read Genesis 11:1-9 to discover the original meaning of the word *Babel*.

1. _____
2. _____
3. _____
4. _____
5. _____
6. _____
7. _____
8. _____
9. _____
10. _____
11. _____
12. _____
13. _____
14. _____
15. _____

16. _____
17. _____
18. _____
19. _____
20. _____
21. _____
22. _____
23. _____
24. _____
25. _____
26. _____
27. _____
28. _____
29. _____
30. _____

BABEL _____

TOWER OF BABEL
Genesis 11:1-9

Directions: Design a monument that exhibits the values of our present society. Explain what parts of this monument God would dislike.

BEGINNINGS REVIEW:
Who's Who

Directions: Identify the following people. Reread Genesis 1:1—11:9 if you need help.

Abel—

Adam—

Cain—

Eve—

Ham—

Japheth—

Noah—

Shem—

Snake—

BEGINNINGS REVIEW:
Word Game

Directions: Fifteen words from this unit are hidden in the puzzle below. While some words may be L-shaped or in other configurations, they are written so that the letters are adjacent. An example is circled.

F	D	G	A	S	L	E	N	K	F
L	O	O	D	P	I	G	H	T	R
B	V	Q	A	M	E	M	K	I	U
G	E	I	R	S	S	O	F	F	A
P	A	R	K	N	O	A	H	E	M
I	M	D	Y	E	G	N	I	R	E
Q	C	X	I	S	P	S	W	E	D
L	O	U	R	S	E	T	O	R	N
F	A	C	E	E	V	H	P	W	A

God
Light
Darkness
Fruit
Adam
Curse
Wanderer
Offering
Ark
Mark (of Cain)
Flood
Tower
Dove
Noah
Blood

Patriarchs

PROMISED LAND

Activity 1

Genesis 11:31-32, 12:1-20, 13:1-18

Directions: The sentences below are events happening to Abram, Lot or both. Place the number of the sentence under the appropriate name(s).

Abram   **Lot**

1. The Lord said that he would bless him and make his name famous.
2. He started out for Canaan.
3. He built an altar to the Lord.
4. The Lord appeared to him.
5. He told Sarai to pretend that she was his sister.
6. He decided that they should separate.
7. He chose land near Sodom on which to settle.
8. God promised to give him many descendants.
9. He was a very rich man.

PROMISED LAND

Genesis 11:31-32, 12:1-20, 13:1-18

Directions: Explain what might have happened to Abram, Sarai and Lot if the following changes were made in the text.

1. There was not a famine in Canaan.

2. Sarai was a very plain looking woman.

3. When Abram entered Egypt, he told the king that Sarai was his wife.

4. God did not send terrible diseases on the people of Egypt.

5. Lot became a high court official in Egypt.

6. Lot did not accompany Abram into Canaan but instead stayed behind in Egypt.

7. Both Abram and Lot wanted the choice land in Canaan.

ISHMAEL'S BIRTH

Genesis 16:1-15

Directions: Record the similarities and differences between each pair of characters.

```
                    ┌──────────────────┐
                    │ 1. Sarai         │
                    │    Hagar         │
        ┌───────────┼──────────────────┼───────────┐
        │ 2. Sarai  │                  │ 4. Abram  │
        │    Ishmael│  SIMILARITIES    │    Sarai  │
        ├───────────┤  AND             ├───────────┤
        │ 3. Hagar  │  DIFFERENCES     │ 5. Abram  │
        │    Ishmael│                  │    Hagar  │
        └───────────┼──────────────────┼───────────┘
                    │ 6. Abram         │
                    │    Ishmael       │
                    └──────────────────┘
```

1. Similarities:

   Differences:

2. Similarities:

   Differences:

3. Similarities:

   Differences:

4. Similarities:

   Differences:

5. Similarities:

   Differences:

6. Similarities:

   Differences:

ISHMAEL'S BIRTH

Activity 4

Genesis 16:1-15

Directions: Evaluate the statements 1 through 6. Check those that you feel are true. Following each statement, explain your reasoning. Then read Genesis 16:1-15.

1. A man should have only one wife.

2. A husband should make decisions for his family.

3. A wife should ask her husband's opinion before making a decision.

4. A family is only complete when there are children.

5. An employer should not mistreat his employees.

6. No one should own slaves.

After reading Genesis 16:1-15, evaluate the statements below. Check those you feel are true. Following each, explain your reasoning.

1. Abram should not have had a child with Hagar.

2. Abram should have controlled Sarai's treatment of Hagar.

3. Sarai was right in asking permission of Abram to treat Hagar as she pleased.

4. Sarai was right to want childen so badly.

6. Sarai should not have treated Hagar unkindly.

7. Abram should have freed Hagar, allowing her to work for his family if she wished.

Note: God changed Abram's name to Abraham and Sarai's name to Sarah (Genesis 17:1-15).

SODOM AND GOMORRAH

Activity 5

Genesis 18:1—19:29

Directions: Read the selection, then close your Bible. Fill in the blanks with whatever word comes to your mind. Each blank represents one word.

Abraham was a very _____ man. When he saw _____

passing by his _____ he ran out to _____ them and asked

them to _____ and _____ while he _____ _____

and _____ them. Sarah baked _____. Abraham ordered a

_____ to prepare a _____ _____ for their _____.

The strangers informed Abraham that Sarah would _____

_____ _____ in _____ _____, an announcement

that _____ the _____ since Sarah was past the age of _____

_____. Sarah also felt _____ at the announcement. The

strangers must have been _____.

Then Abraham _____ the strangers to a place where they could

look down on _____. At this time the Lord decided to take

_____ into his confidence. The Lord told _____ that the people

of Sodom and _____ were _____ and that He planned to

_____ the towns. Abraham felt _____ at the news and

_____ the Lord. Abraham was _____ to speak to the Lord and

ask questions in regard to Sodom and Gomorrah.

Lot, like _____, offered to serve the _____ who came to town. They went with Lot to his _____. The men of Sodom made _____ advances and Lot _____ them not to be so _____. All the men who came to Lot's house were made _____. Lot was _____ by the _____ to leave Sodom. So Lot _____ his family together in order to _____. Lot was _____ to leave, but the Lord felt _____ and _____ him. Lot was probably spared because of his _____. The _____ ordered the family not to look back. Lot's wife, a very _____ woman, did look back and was turned into a _____ _____ _____. The next day Sodom and Gomorrah were only _____ in the desert.

SODOM AND GOMORRAH   Activity 6

Genesis 18:1 —19:29

Directions: As a newspaper reporter, write the *scoops* for the following headlines. Information comes from Genesis 18:1—19:29

SKY RAINS FIRE

ABRAHAM BARTERS WITH GOD

GUESTS FIND TOWN FAR FROM HOSPITABLE

NEW MONUMENT TO BE DEDICATED IN DESERT

ABRAHAM'S TEST   Activity 7

Genesis 21:1-21, 22:1-19

Directions: Put the following events in chronological order on the time line by placing the appropriate letters above the notches.

A—Isaac carries wood for the sacrifice.
B—Isaac asks where the sacrifice is.
C—Sarah bears a son and names him Isaac.
D—God shows Hagar a well.
E—Ishmael and Isaac pray together.
F—Sarah demands that Hagar and Ishmael be sent away.

G—Hagar wanders in the wilderness and expects to die.
H—Ishmael cries.
I—God tells Abraham to take Isaac to Moriah and offer him as a sacrifice.
J—Abraham leaves the donkey with the servant.
K—An angel of the Lord calls down and stops Abraham.
L—Abraham tells Isaac that God will provide a lamb for the sacrifice.

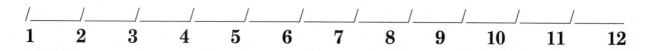

```
/_____/_____/_____/_____/_____/_____/_____/_____/_____/_____/_____/_____/
1     2      3      4      5      6      7      8      9      10     11     12
```

ABRAHAM'S TEST

Activity 8

Genesis 21:1-21, 22:1-19

Directions: Imagine that you are Sarah, Hagar, Abraham or Isaac. Answer the questions as if you were being interviewed by a gossip columnist.

SARAH INTERVIEW

Why did you decide to send Hagar to Abraham?

Was Abraham interested in Hagar before this? When did you decide this could be more than a passing fancy? Please describe the incident to us.

Did you or Abraham want children? Why were children so important to your marriage?

Please describe Hagar. What kinds of friends did she have? What were some of her irritating habits? What was her family like?

When did you decide to send Hagar into the desert? Why? Didn't you feel guilty about this?

Where do you think Hagar went after this? What do you think happened to her?

What was her son, Ishmael, like? How did he get along with Isaac?

Is your home life better now that Hagar is gone? Please explain.

HAGAR INTERVIEW

What was it like being Abraham's concubine?

Did he love you better than he loved Sarah? Why? Why not?

What duties did you do in the home that Sarah refused to do?

Can you remember one of the fights Sarah and Abraham had? What was it about? Please describe it.

What was Sarah really like? What kinds of friends did Sarah have? What did she do in her spare time?

Why did Sarah *really* resent you? Did this begin before she sent you into Abraham? Perhaps you could recount one of the fights the two of you had.

How did Isaac and Ishmael get along?

What was your life like after your departure from Abraham's household?

ABRAHAM INTERVIEW

What made you think that God really spoke to you? Could you see him? What did he look like? What did his voice sound like?

What kind of a God would demand that you kill your son? Why did he do it?

Did you believe that Sarah would have other children?

What was Sarah's reaction to what happened? Did she know what you were going to do when you left home? What did she say when you returned home?

What were your friends' reactions when you told them about the experience? Please explain this in detail for our readers.

How did this experience affect Isaac?

Just out of curiosity, did you really love Sarah more than Hagar? Why did you let Sarah talk you into letting Hagar go? (People have called you henpecked for that, you know.)

ISAAC INTERVIEW

What have you done with your life since that mountaintop experience?

What did your father tell you on the way up the mountain? When did you actually realize what was happening?

Tell us about your feelings at the time. When did you become frightened? Can you remember the conversation between yourself and your father at the time? (That would be most interesting to the readers.)

Do you think your father would have sacrificed you if the angel hadn't stopped him?

Did your father really see an angel, or did he just imagine it? Explain exactly what you saw and heard.

Do you resent your father for being willing to kill you?

How did the experience affect your life?

Explain how your relationship with your father changed after this.

Off the record, what did you think of Hagar and Ishmael?

BIRTHRIGHT

Genesis 25:19-34, 27:1-45

Directions: Think about family relationships in the story, of the rivalry between Jacob and Esau (Genesis 25:19-34, 27:1-45). Explain characters' feelings or views about each other in the spaces below. Find passages that support your ideas.

1. Rebecca views Esau:

2. Rebecca views Jacob:

3. Rebecca views Isaac:

4. Isaac views Esau:

5. Isaac views Jacob:

6. Jacob views Esau:

7. Esau views Jacob:

BIRTHRIGHT

Genesis 25:19-34, 27:1-45

Directions: In the circles list qualities and outstanding words or deeds of Jacob and Esau. In the overlapping area, list qualities or characteristics that Esau and Jacob have in common.

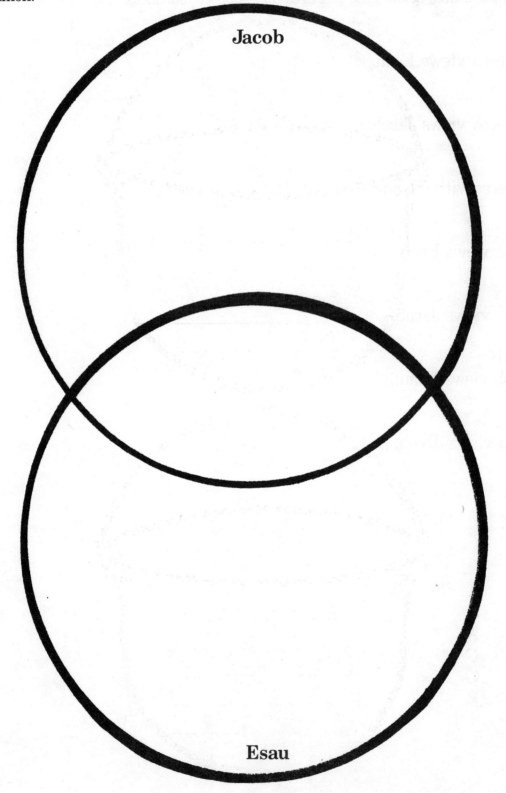

LABAN'S DECEPTION

Genesis 29:1-30

Activity 11

Directions: Put into the kettles the essential ingredients making up the personalities and relationships of Laban and Jacob.

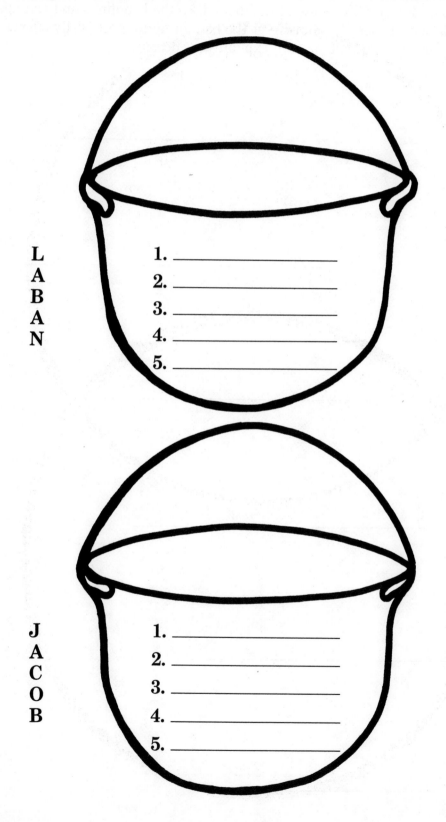

L
A
B
A
N

1. _____
2. _____
3. _____
4. _____
5. _____

J
A
C
O
B

1. _____
2. _____
3. _____
4. _____
5. _____

LABAN'S DECEPTION

Activity 12

Genesis 29:1-30

Directions: Before reading Genesis 29:1-30, cut out six articles from newspapers or magazines that are representative of deception in America today. Consider which deceptions you consider morally worse than others. Clip the headlines and arrange them in ascending order (least morally offensive at the bottom up to most orally offensive at the top). Keep the articles so that you can explain your decisions.

_____

_____

_____

_____

_____

_____

JACOB'S DECEPTION

Activity 13

Genesis 30:25-43, 31:1-3, 31:17-21, 33:18-20

Directions: Fill in each line below with a word describing an emotion or feeling between the characters connected by the line.

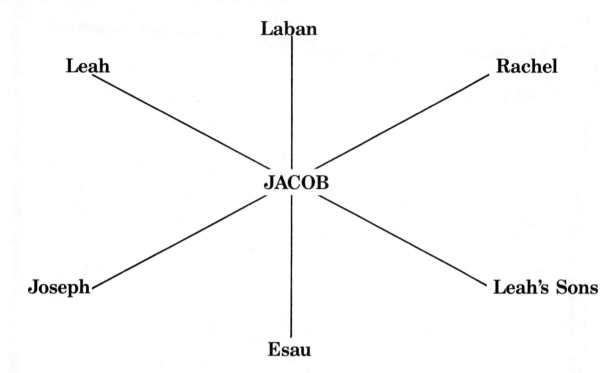

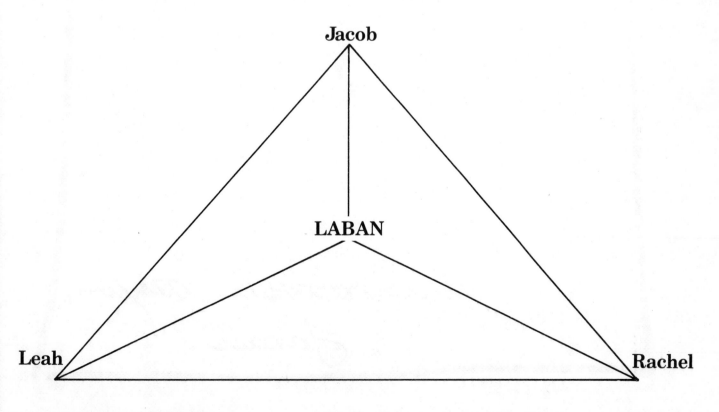

JACOB'S DECEPTION

Genesis 30:25-43, 31:1-3, 31:17-21, 33:18-20

Directions: Assuming that you are Laban and that Ur has a local newspaper, write a letter to your neighbors asking for help in regaining your stolen goods (including your daughters!).

Dear friends,

a respectable citizen,
Laban

PATRIARCHS REVIEW:
Who's Who

Directions: Identify the following people. Reread Genesis 11:31—33:20 if you need help.

Abraham—

Hagar—

Isaac—

Ishmael—

Jacob—

Laban—

Leah—

Lot—

Rachel—

Rebecca—

Sarah—

Terah

PATRIARCHS REVIEW:
Word Game

Activity 16

Directions: Find the answers to the questions below. Answers will be written horizontally, vertically and diagonally. Reread Genesis 11:31—33:20 if you need help.

```
V  H  C  C  A  K  I  P  A  O  V  E  B  E  T  L  N  C
S  L  A  M  B  O  U  Y  V  W  Y  X  T  Y  E  M  Q  A
X  K  U  A  B  P  K  L  E  A  N  I  S  A  R  A  H  P
D  R  N  S  T  H  O  I  N  O  R  I  O  H  S  T  O  Z
Z  F  F  R  C  P  D  E  S  C  E  N  D  A  N  T  S  C
T  Q  E  S  S  O  T  G  D  H  W  O  O  D  L  I  H  L
J  P  A  N  E  R  H  Y  L  A  M  B  M  I  B  I  E  A
E  M  I  J  K  R  L  P  E  T  F  A  R  G  S  T  P  X
I  E  S  S  N  I  A  T  E  R  H  T  E  N  C  T  H  X
O  F  F  L  E  D  A  I  S  E  U  F  S  L  Y  U  E  V
H  O  P  E  L  G  H  A  G  A  R  H  A  N  D  O  R  W
H  O  H  M  M  E  T  N  U  I  C  I  U  L  S  N  D  W
E  G  P  N  H  O  P  G  S  F  G  O  P  U  E  B  I  H
N  F  A  N  L  R  O  E  C  Y  J  H  E  N  G  B  O  O
I  H  M  O  L  E  E  L  D  B  T  J  H  K  L  I  S  K
M  I  S  M  N  K  E  S  A  F  O  U  R  T  E  E  N  Y
```

1. What did God promise to Abraham?
2. What city did Abraham come from?
3. What king desired Sarah?
4. What city did Lot choose as his home?
5. Who was childless?
6. Who became proud because she was pregnant?
7. Who would live like a donkey, apart from relatives?
8. God said he would not destroy Sodom if as few as _____ people were righteous.
9. Who led Lot and his family out of Sodom?
10. When on the mountain, what did Abraham say God would supply?
11. What did Isaac carry up the mountain?
12. Which of Isaac's sons was a hunter?
13. What did Jacob buy Esau's birthright with?
14. How many years did Jacob work for Rachel?
15. In what capacity did Jacob work for Laban?

Migration to Egypt

JOSEPH SOLD INTO SLAVERY Activity 1
Genesis 37:1-36

Directions: Which character(s) would most likely have written the following ads?

WANTED: Excellent material suitable for a decorative robe. Contact:	**FOR SALE:** Young man who has big dreams. Twenty pieces of silver. Firm price. Contact:
WANTED: Qualified psychiatrist or dream analyst to help rid loved one of delusions of grandeur. Contact:	**WANTED:** Whereabouts of brother known to have been trapped in well. Contact:
LOST: Shepherd last believed to be tending flock in area of Shechem. Contact:	**WANTED:** A robe and a goat. Will make good offer. Contact:
WANTED: Fearless personality to assist brothers in eliminating a bothersome problem. Contact:	**INFORMATION NEEDED:** Last known whereabouts of Joseph. Believed attacked by wild animals. Contact:
WANTED: Location of some dry wells. Contact:	**WANTED:** Slave to serve in noble capacity. Anyone having captured a suitable prospect, Contact:

JOSEPH SOLD INTO SLAVERY

Activity 2

Genesis 37:1-36

Directions: In the style of a lawyer, defend Joseph's brothers before the court where they have been indicted for the kidnapping of their brother. Keep in mind Jacob's preference for Joseph and do not be afraid to appeal to the emotions of the jury.

Your Honor, distinguished ladies and gentlemen, while I will admit that my clients are guilty, there are extenuating circumstances. . . .

JOSEPH AND POTIPHAR'S WIFE

Activity 3

Genesis 39:2-23

Directions: Mark the fact statements (F) and the opinion statements (O).

____ 1. Joseph missed his father and family while held captive in Egypt.

____ 2. Joseph's success caused him to be proud.

____ 3. Joseph's work for Potiphar was enjoyable.

____ 4. The Lord made Joseph successful in serving Potiphar.

____ 5. Joseph was Potiphar's personal servant.

____ 6. Joseph was in charge of all of Potiphar's concerns.

____ 7. Joseph was attractive to Potiphar's wife.

____ 8. Being attractive caused problems for Joseph.

____ 9. Potiphar's wife was interested in Joseph.

____ 10. Potiphar's wife should not have flirted with Joseph.

____ 11. Potiphar's wife felt embarrassed when Joseph refused her.

____ 12. Joseph refused to be immoral.

____ 13. Joseph was framed by Potiphar's wife.

____ 14. Potiphar's wife committed a worse crime against Joseph than against her husband.

____ 15. Potiphar believed his wife's accusations.

____ 16. Considering Joseph's loyalty, Potiphar was wrong to believe his wife.

____ 17. Almost any man would believe his wife over a servant.

____ 18. Almost any man would believe that finding another man's clothing in his room would be very incriminating.

____ 19. Joseph was well-liked by his jailers.

____ 20. Joseph should have sought revenge against Potiphar's wife.

JOSEPH AND POTIPHAR'S WIFE

Activity 4

Genesis 39:2-23

Directions: Write two limericks, one about Joseph and the other about Potiphar's wife.

Example: There once was a woman, a tease,
Who said, "Won't you sleep with me, please?"
But Joseph, appalled,
Said, "No, not at all!"
So she sent for the guards, crying, "Seize!"

There once was a man _____

_____

_____

_____

_____

There once was a woman _____

_____

_____

_____

_____

DREAMS

Genesis 40:1-23, 41:1-57

Directions: Circle the word or phrase that is *not* associated with the clue in the Biblical passage.

clue: **wine steward**

    prison   grapes   execution   dream

clue: **baker**

    prison   vine   birds   hanging

clue: **birthday**

    dream   banquet   king   execution

clue: **thin cows**

    Nile River   appetite   famine   eight

clue: **ripe grain**

    famine   seven   dream   swallowed

clue: **Joseph**

    ring   governor   jewels   chariot

clue: **Arsenath**

    king's daughter   wife   Manasseh   Joseph

clue: **dreams**

    fat cows   ripe grain   grape press   breadbasket

DREAMS

Genesis 40:1-23, 41:1-57

Directions: Put the following people or items under the appropriate category headings below. Then, make up five headings of your own and group items under each one.

wine steward
chief baker
captain of
  the guard
King of Egypt
Joseph
magicians
wise men
two
three
seven
life
prison
dreams
grapevine
king's cup
breadbaskets
bird
head
cows
heads of grain
reserve supply
linen robe
ring
gold chain
royal chariot
wife
children
governor
prisoner
famine
plenty

1. **Dreamers**

2. **Prisoners**

3. **Interpreters**

4. **Leaders**

5. **Symbols**

6. **Rewards**

7. **Punishments**

8. **Prophecies**

9. **Lost**

10. **Numbers found
   in dreams**

_____

11. _____   14. _____

12. _____   15. _____

13. _____

SIMEON HELD HOSTAGE

Activity 7

Genesis 42:1-38

Directions: Fill in the wheels of emotion and reason for both Joseph and his brothers. Between each spoke fill in the emotions each felt as reflected in Genesis 42:1-38. Also, give the reasons for their feelings.

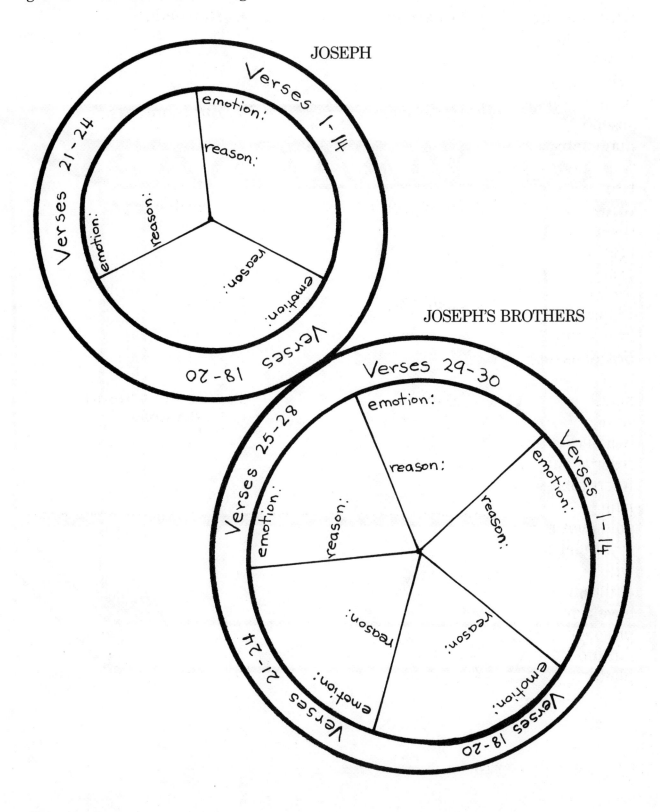

Copyright © 1984, Winston Press, Inc.

43

SIMEON HELD HOSTAGE

Activity 8

Genesis 42:1-38

Directions: Below is a picture of a stage. The people and objects from the Scripture selection have been omitted. Draw them on the stage.

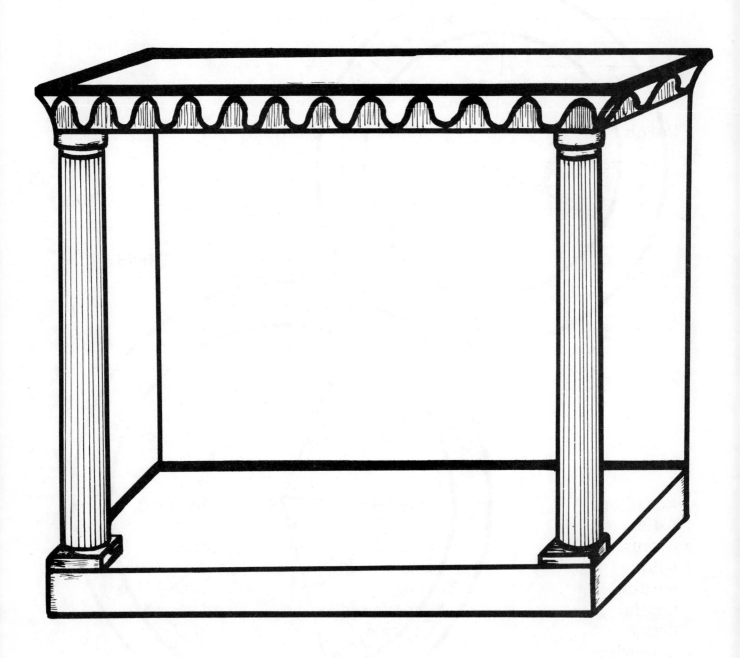

STOLEN CUP

Genesis 43:1-34, 44:1-13

Activity 9

Directions: Listed below are descriptive words. Use at least three that describe *opposite* qualities of the heading. Be prepared to explain your choices.

the famine

1 _____

2 _____

3 _____

Benjamin

1 _____

2 _____

3 _____

Jacob

1 _____

2 _____

3 _____

the brothers

1 _____

2 _____

3 _____

Judah

1 _____

2 _____

3 _____

the Egyptians

1 _____

2 _____

3 _____

unwilling
patient
untrustworthy
willing
trusting
hopeful
better
improving

happy
plentiful
unloved
oldest
stingy
unprotected
unafraid

dishonest
hard-hearted
humble
poor
unprepared
dead
ill

STOLEN CUP

Activity 10

Genesis 43:1-34, 44:1-13

Directions: You are working on the *Egyptian Herald*. Your job is to raise the paper's circulation by printing *spicy* headlines. For each group of verses, write a headline that would encourage readers to buy your paper rather than the competitor's paper.

Genesis 43:1-14 (reprinted from the *Canaanite Gazette*)

Genesis 43:15-17

Genesis 43:18-23

Genesis 43:24-34

Genesis 44:1-13

JOSEPH AND JACOB REUNITED

Activity 11

Genesis 44:14-34, 45:1-28, 46:1-6

Directions: Reread the verses beside each name to determine the person's outstanding characteristics. Using this information, fill in the blanks, making original comparisons.
Example: Joseph
       as *unbending* as *steel*

Jacob (Genesis 37:3-4, 45:21-46:7)

as _____ as _____

as _____ as _____

Joseph (Genesis 37:5-11, 39:6-23, 41:25-49, 42:6-17, 45:1-20)

as _____ as _____

as _____ as _____

as _____ as _____

as _____ as _____

Judah (Genesis 37:25-28, 44:18-34)

as _____ as _____

as _____ as _____

Pharaoh (Genesis 41:37-45, 45:16-20)

as _____ as _____

Benjamin (Genesis 43:26-34, 44:18-34)

as _____ as _____

JACOB AND JOSEPH REUNITED

Activity 12

Genesis 44:14-34, 45:1-28, 46:1-6

Directions: Write telegrams from the following people to be sent to Jacob. Do not use more than 10 words for each telegram.

Judah

NILE UNION

To:

Message:

Sender:

Joseph

NILE UNION

To:

Message:

Sender:

Pharaoh

NILE UNION

To:

Message:

Sender:

Benjamin

NILE UNION

To:

Message:

Sender:

Reuben

NILE UNION

To:

Message:

Sender:

Simeon

NILE UNION

To:

Message:

Sender:

MIGRATION TO EGYPT
REVIEW: Who's Who

Directions: Identify the following people. Reread Genesis 37—46:10 if you need help.

Baker—

Benjamin—

Jacob—

Joseph—

Judah—

King of Egypt—

Potiphar—

Potiphar's wife—

Reuben—

Simeon—

Wine steward—

MIGRATION TO EGYPT
REVIEW: Game

Directions: Make twenty-five 2″ × 3″ cards. Write a question and answer on one side of each card. Turn the cards face down on your side of the board. Make a game token and place it in the *Canaan* square opposite your opponent's *Canaan* square.

Wilderness

MOSES' BIRTH   Activity 1
Exodus 1:1-22, 2:1-10

Directions: For the following newspaper headline, write three *different* news stories that would apply to Exodus 1:1-22, 2:1-10.

FEAR CAUSES STRANGE OCCURRENCE

FEAR CAUSES STRANGE OCCURRENCE

FEAR CAUSES STRANGE OCCURRENCE

MOSES' BIRTH

Activity 2

Exodus 1:1-25, 2:1-10

Directions: Answer the questions below by filling in the blanks with an answer from one of the spaces in the grid following the questions. Blacken the spaces in the grid as you use the answers inside. If you answer all the questions correctly you should see a shape when you are finished. Explain the meaning of the shape in the space provided.

1. How many descendants did Jacob have in Egypt? _____
2. Name Jacob's sons who went to Egypt. _____

_____   _____   _____   _____

_____   _____   _____   _____

_____   _____

3. Which of Jacob's sons was already in Egypt? _____
4. The new king of Egypt feared which group because they were numerous and strong? _____
5. What did the Egyptians do to suppress this group? _____
6. The midwives were ordered to kill whom? _____
7. How long did Moses' mother hide him? _____
8. What item did Moses' mother make to save her child? _____
9. What had Moses' mother done to the item in the previous question to make it safe? _____
10. Where did Moses' mother put him? _____
11. Who watched Moses to see what would happen to him? _____
12. Who found Moses? _____
13. What were the names of the midwives? _____
14. Who supposedly gave birth easily? _____
15. Which river were the children to be thrown into? _____
16. Which cities were built for the king? _____
17. For what purpose were they built? _____
18. Why had the king's daughter gone to the river? _____
19. Who was chosen to care for Moses after he had been found? _____
20. Who accompanied the princess to the river bank? _____
21. When Moses was old enough, what did the king's daughter do?

_____

22. What did the princess offer to do for Moses' mother? _____
23. What did Moses' name mean? _____

24. The king was worried that in case of war, Moses' people might join up with whom?_____

25. Because the midwives did not kill the babies, God granted them what?_____

26. What substance was used to make Moses' basket safe for the river?_____

imprison / Naphtali	king's wife / love	twenty / blankets	fishing / friends	protection / Hittites	Obadiah / Benjamin
Judah / adopted him	hate / tar	Joshua / long life	teenagers / leaves	denied him / slaves	supply centers / bathe
Israelites / Shiphrah	Zebulum / Puah	girl babies / Ramses	exiled him / mother	Issachar / basket of reeds	boy babies / families
Asher / Pithom	tall grass by river / chosen one	Joseph / seventy	hard labor / waterproof	Dan / secret panel	Gad / enemies
king's daughter / Nile	Michael / punished	sister / leader	Simeon / food	fifty / Canaanites	three months / pull out
Hebrew women / Levi	king's son / one year	mother / Jeremiah	six months / king	Amos / killed him	pay her / Reuben

Explanation of shape: _____

THE BURNING BUSH Activity 3

Exodus 2:11-25, 3:1-15

Directions: Fill in the situations in this Situation/Consequence worksheet. The consequences are given. Try to think backwards and determine what situation caused the consequence.

1. **Situation—**
   Consequence—Moses killed the Egyptian and hid the body.

2. **Situation—**
   Consequence—A Hebrew man asked if Moses was going to kill him.

3. **Situation—**
   Consequence—The king tried to have Moses killed.

4. **Situation—**
   Consequence—Moses fled to the land of Midian.

5. **Situation—**
   Consequence—Moses was invited to dinner by Jethro.

6. **Situation—**
   Consequence—God spoke to Moses.

7. **Situation—**
   Consequence—Moses covered his face.

8. **Situation—**
   Consequence—Moses told God that he didn't feel worthy enough for the task.

9. **Situation—**
   Consequence—God announced his name.

THE BURNING BUSH

Activity 4

Exodus 2:11-25, 3:1-15

Directions: Assume that God held a press conference about the events described in Exodus 2:11-25—3:1-15. What ten questions would you ask of God?

1.

2.

3.

4.

5.

6.

7.

8.

9.

10.

PLAGUES

Exodus 6:28—11:10

Directions: Before reading Exodus 6:28—11:10, write a descriptive scene using the following words. Create the mood they suggest.

sores
hunger
death
stench
no escape

PLAGUES

Exodus 6:28—11:10

Directions: Write an editorial in the local newspaper in which you, an average Egyptian citizen, express your concerns over the alarming happenings of the past few weeks. Your editorial should mention the major disasters endured and your reactions to them.

ESCAPE FROM EGYPT

Activity 7

Exodus 12:29-42, 13:17—14:31

Directions: Decide upon the chronological order of these events. All odd numbers are found in column A and all even numbers are found in column B.

Column A	Column B
____The pillar of cloud followed the Israelites.	____The Israelites baked unleavened bread.
____The Egyptian soldiers panicked.	____The Israelites complained to Moses.
____Pharaoh told Moses to leave.	____The Egyptians gave dough to the Israelites.
____The sea became dry land.	____The sea covered the Egyptian army.
____Pharaoh's son died.	____The Israelites camped at Etham.
____The Israelites started on their journey.	____Moses held his hand over the sea for the first time.
____The Israelites camped at Sukkoth.	____The Egyptians cried for the dead.
____Pharaoh pursued the Israelites.	____The Israelites walked into the sea.

ESCAPE FROM EGYPT

Activity 8

Exodus 12:29-42, 13:17—14:31

Directions: Unscramble the hypothetical newspaper headlines below.

MAIFLSEI ROUMN OSSN

SIARESITLE AECPES THIW LLAAVURSE

YPEGNTIA RAMY RUSSPUE SIARESITLE

OGD RAPTS HET ERD ESA

RAMY WDRSNO NI ERD ESA

LNDEUEVNAE DAERB TSERLU OF UQCKI VOEM

DOYB OF SOJHPE OT EB RUBEID GAAIN

LIPLAR OF RIFE ESNE NI SYK

FOOD FOR THE ISRAELITES   Activity 9

Exodus 16:1-31

Directions: Read the Scripture selection to play the game below. The teacher will explain the rules of play.

Start	The Israelite community set out from _____.	They complained to Moses that they were _____	The Lord told Moses He would _____ from Heaven.	**?**
The Israelites journeyed for _____ years until they reached Canaan.				_____told his people that the Lord would provide.
Moses commanded _____ to save a sample of the food for posterity.				A large flock of _____ flew into camp.
The people called the food from the Lord _____.				In the morning food was also found _____.
On the seventh day some of the people disobeyed and _____.				Each person was told to gather _____ (amount)
?	The seventh day was commanded to be the day _____	On the sixth day the people gathered _____	People who collected too much food	Israelites were told not to _____

FOOD FOR THE ISRAELITES Activity 10

Exodus 16:1-31

Directions: Choose pictures from a magazine to place on this page taken from an Israelite's scrapbook. It should represent his journey so far. Remember that the journey began with the Passover.

THE TEN COMMANDMENTS Activity 11

Exodus 19:1-3, 20:1-17, 32:1-35

Directions: Eight of the Ten Commandments are written in negative terms. Rewrite them positively to express what the Israelites *should* do, rather than what they should *not* do. Note the two commandments that are already written in positive terms.

1. You shall not have any other gods before me.

2. You shall not make a graven image.

3. You shall not take the name of the Lord, your God, in vain.

4. Remember the sabbath day, to keep it holy.

5. Honor your father and your mother.

6. You shall not kill.

7. You shall not commit adultery.

8. You shall not steal.

9. You shall not bear false witness against your neighbor.

10. You shall not covet.

THE TEN COMMANDMENTS Activity 12

Exodus 19:1-3, 20:1-17, 32:1-35

Directions: Make a list of *commandments* you follow. These may be rules you set for yourself or rules others set for you.

1.

2.

3.

4.

5.

6.

7.

8.

9.

10.

DISSATISFACTION   Activity 13

Numbers 13:1-33, 14:1-37

Directions: Moses and his people each have forty dollars to spend at the marketplace. What do you think they would buy from the list below? Your choices should reflect the values and concerns of the characters.

$10 A Life of Security Back in Egypt
$10 Obedience to God
$10 Faith in God's Protection
$10 Enough to Eat
$10 Fear of God's Power
$10 Knowing what the Future Holds

$10 More than Enough to Eat
$10 Protection from the Canaanites
$10 A Better Leader
$10 A Guarantee of Reaching Canaan

Moses' Choices

1.
2.
3.
4.

People's Choices

1.
2.
3.
4.

DISSATISFACTION

Numbers 13:1-33, 14:1-37

Activity 14

Directions: Below is a symbol of the promised land: grapes taken from Canaan. The promised land, however, was unreachable for forty years because of the Israelites' fears. In each of the circles, write down one of your own fears.

DEATH OF MOSES

Activity 15

Numbers 20:2-12, 21:4-9, Deuteronomy 34:1-12

Directions: Write want-ads similar to those in the personal section of the newspaper.

WANTED by Highest Authority

WANTED:

Contact Moses

WANTED by the people of Israel

Contact P of I Headquarters

WANTED:

Aaron

DEATH OF MOSES

Numbers 20:2-12, 21:4-9 Deuteronomy 34:1-12

Directions: Choose the correct path to Canaan.

WILDERNESS
REVIEW: Who's Who

Activity 17

Directions: Identify the following people. Reread the Scripture quotes from Chapter 4 if you need help.

Aaron—

Caleb—

Jethro—

Joshua—

Moses—

Zipporah—

WILDERNESS
REVIEW: Crossword Puzzle   Activity 18

Directions: Answer the crossword puzzle questions by filling in the correct word or words in the appropriate spaces.

ACROSS

4. God engraved his commandments on two stone _____.

5. On their way out of Egypt, the Israelites took one food item, _____.

8. The mysterious food God sent was called _____.

9. Moses sent some men to _____ in Canaan.

14. Who did the king fear because they were so numerous?

17. Who rescued Moses? (two words)

19. Jethro gave Moses his daughter, _____.

20. Moses was hidden in a basket of _____.

23. The name of the holy mountain.

24. The king demanded that all newborn Hebrew _____ be killed.

25. The Lord gave the Israelites water out of a _____.

26. A word to describe the Egyptian king.

28. The Israelites carried away the _____ of the Egyptians on their way out.

29. Moses and Aaron used ashes from the furnace to cause _____ on people and animals.

30. A pillar of _____ gave the travelers light to travel by at night.

DOWN

1. The Israelites traveled through the desert for _____ years.

2. One of the twelve spies who survived God's punishment was _____.

3. The Israelites eventually settled in _____.

6. What body of water did the Israelites cross? (two words)

7. The Israelites were pursued by the _____ on their way out.

10. Moses fled to _____.

11. Who told Moses and Aaron to leave the country?

12. A type of bird the Lord sent to the Israelites to feed them in the desert.

13. Moses killed a/an _____.

15. A word that describes Egyptian oppression and forced hard labor.

16. One thing Moses saw on top of the mountain. (2 words)

18. The Israelites made a bull out of _____.

22. In addition to the plagues and other disasters, the Lord declared that in every household the _____ would die. (two words)

26. Aaron turned the walking stick into a _____.

27. Aaron turned the river water into _____.

Promised Land

ESPIONAGE IN JERICHO
Joshua 1:1-18, 2:1-24

Activity 1

Directions: A scroll has been found with a contract setting forth the terms of negotiation between Rahab and the spies. Complete the terms of the contract below.

I, Rahab of Jericho, do swear

Rahab

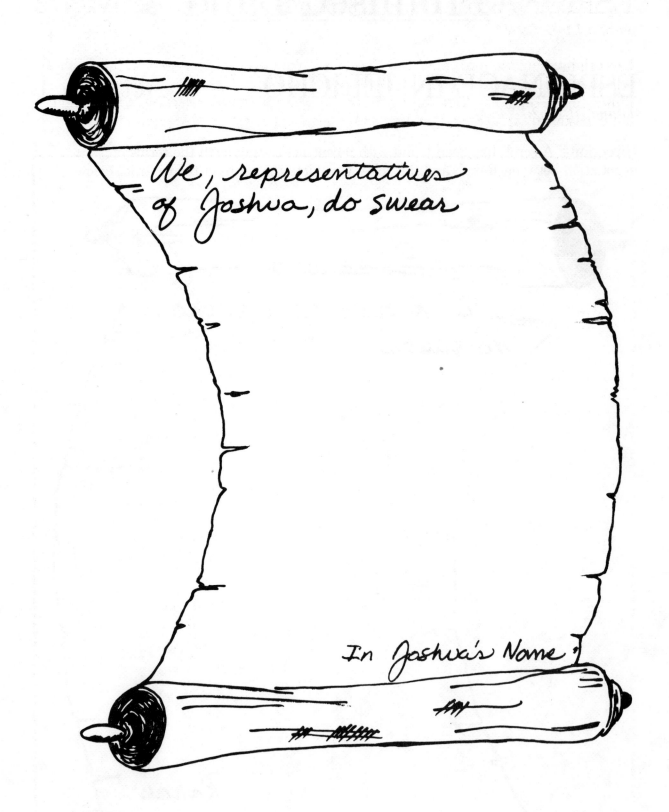

We, representatives of Joshua, do swear

In Joshua's Name

ESPIONAGE IN JERICHO

Activity 2

Joshua 1:1-18, 2:1-24

Directions: Imagine that you are in charge of promoting a movie based on this Biblical
selection. Do these three things: (1) Give the movie a title, (2) Design a poster
illustrating a key scene from the movie, (3) Write a one sentence caption at the bottom
of the poster to capture the attention and interest of the potential viewers.

DESTRUCTION OF JERICHO   Activity 3
Joshua 6:1-27

Directions: Write a eulogy that would have been appropriate upon Joshua's death. Then, write a eulogy that you think would be appropriate for yourself.

Eulogy for Joshua

Eulogy for _____

OPPRESSION OF THE ISRAELITES
Activity 4
Judges 2:6-23, 3:1-31, 4:1-24

Directions: In recent times many celebrities have been writing their autobiographies. Think of original titles for the autobiographies or biographies of the following people.

Joshua—

Othniel—

Ehud—

Deborah—

Barak—

Sisera—

Jael—

OPPRESSION
OF THE ISRAELITES

Judges 2:6-23, 3:1-30, 4:1-24

Directions: Write ads that might have appeared in the newspaper during the time of Ehud and Deborah.

Example: WANTED: one left-handed male. Must be good with sword.

LOST:	BUSINESS OPPORTUNITY:
FREE CONSULTATION:	**USED:**
MESSAGE FOR:	**WILLING TO SELL:**
WANTED:	**DEAL ON:**
FOR RENT:	**WISH TO BUY:**

GIDEON

Judges 6:1-40, 7:1-23

Directions: Answer the multiple choice questions by writing the letter of the correct answer in the blank provided. Afterwards, total the number of "A answers," "B answers," and "C answers." You should have the same number of "B answers" as "C answers."

____ 1. During the time of Gideon, the Israelites were bothered by A. the Moabites B. the Midianites C. the Ammonites.

____ 2. Gideon belonged to the tribe of A. Manasseh B. Judah C. Levi.

____ 3. The townspeople wanted to kill Gideon for A. building an altar B. losing the battle C. destroying an altar.

____ 4. Gideon's father was A. Purah B. Hazor C. Joash.

____ 5. When the angel appeared to Gideon, he was A. pressing wine B. threshing wheat C. harvesting barley.

____ 6. The angel said that he had appeared because A. God would punish the Israelites B. God was tired of the Israelites worshipping foreign gods C. God was concerned about the Israelites.

____ 7. Gideon's first response to the angel's message was one of anger expressed toward A. the Israelites B. God C. himself.

____ 8. Gideon responded to his first encounter with God by A. killing God's enemies B. naming the location after God C. building an altar.

____ 9. The foreign gods mentioned in the selection did not include: A. Asherah B. Dagon C. Baal.

____ 10. Gideon asked God for proof that he would help him A. two times B. three times C. four times.

____ 11. Gideon asked for proof in the form of all *except* A. fire B. dew C. dreams.

____ 12. Just over half of Gideon's army went home because A. God had a plan that needed less people B. God wanted to show his power C. those people drank water directly from the river.

____ 13. Gideon gained confidence to attack the camp because of A. a dream B. God's assurance that he would not help Gideon's enemies C. a witch's prophecy.

____ 14. Gideon's army was given all except A. trumpets B. fire C. copies of the Ten Commandments.

"A answers"____   "B answers"____   "C answers"____

GIDEON

Judges 6:1-40, 7:1-23

Directions: Agree (**A**) or disagree (**D**) with the following statements.

_____ 1. God punished the Israelites by allowing the Midianites to oppress them.

_____ 2. The Midianites knew how to hurt the Israelites.

_____ 3. God had a right to be angry with the Israelites.

_____ 4. Gideon had no doubts about following God's directions.

_____ 5. An older son from a prestigious family would have been a better choice for God's purpose than Gideon.

_____ 6. When Gideon destroyed the altar to Baal, the reaction of the townspeople was understandable.

_____ 7. God wanted to receive credit for helping the Israelites destroy the Midianites.

_____ 8. Gideon should not have tested God.

_____ 9. Gideon was a brave soldier.

_____ 10. Gideon's father did not believe in the power of Baal.

SAMSON'S MARRIAGE

Activity 8

Judges 13:1-25, 14:1-20, 15:1-20, 16:1-4

Directions: Each line represents a continuum of emotions from one extreme to another. After reading the statements about the selection, place an "x" on the line to indicate where you feel the character's emotions lie. Explain the reason for your choice.

Manoah and his wife saw the angel of the Lord and heard that they would have a son.

1. /_____/
   unafraid   afraid

2. /_____/
   happy   unhappy

Explanation:

Manoah and his wife responded to Samson's desire to marry a Philistine girl.

3. /_____/
   happy   unhappy

Explanation:

The Philistines tried to figure out Samson's riddle.

4. /_____/
   curious   angry

Explanation:

Samson's wife was threatened by the Philistines.

5. /_____/
   unafraid   afraid

Explanation:

Samson found out that his wife told the answer to the riddle.

6. /_____/
    sympathetic   angry

Explanation:

Samson was informed that his wife had been given to another man.

7. /_____/
    accepting   angry

Explanation:

The Philistines discovered that their wheat crop had been destroyed.

8. /_____/
    unhappy   angry

Explanation:

Samson heard that the Philistines had killed his wife and burned down her father's house.

9. /_____/
    unhappy   angry

Explanation:

Samson was handed over to the Philistines.

10. /_____/
    accepting   violent

Explanation:

SAMSON'S MARRIAGE

Activity 9

Judges 13:1-25, 14:1-20, 15:1-20, 16:1-4

Directions: Write a week's synopses for the television serial entitled, "Samson's Encounters." It is a combination of adventure series and soap opera. While the serial is set in twentieth century New York City, "Samson's Encounters" should be true to character.

Monday
2:30 **Samson's Encounters**

Tuesday
2:30 **Samson's Encounters**

Wednesday
2:30 **Samson's Encounters**

Thursday
2:30 **Samson's Encounters**

Friday
2:30 **Samson's Encounters**

Judges 16:4-31

Directions: Opportunists have decided to open a travel agency after Samson's death. You have been asked to write a travel brochure enticing tourists to the area.

Visit The Land Of The Legend

Yes, you too can visit the birthplace of Samson!

SAMSON AND DELILAH

Judges 16:4-31

Directions: Finish filling in signposts on the map that will accompany a travel brochure.

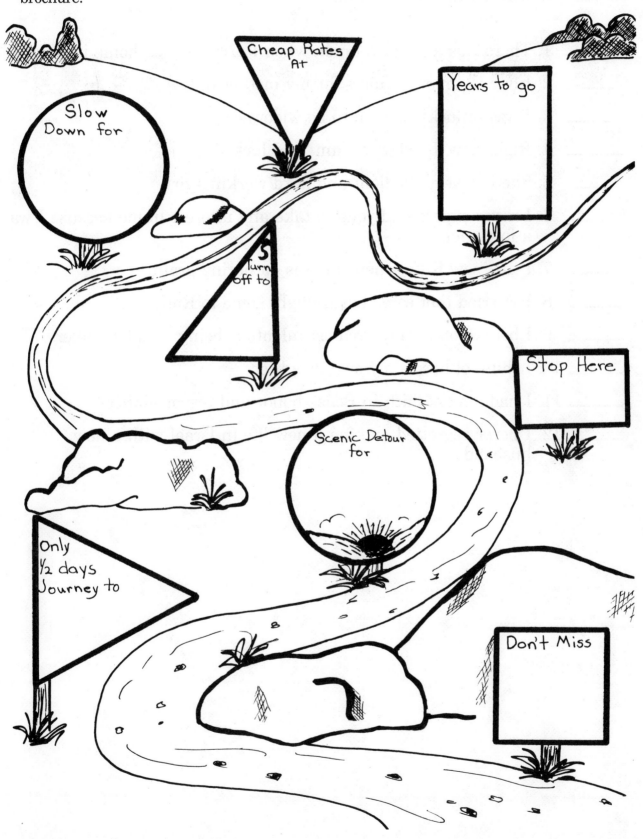

Ruth 1:1—4:22

Directions: Which character or characters might have made the following statements? Choose from Ruth, Boaz, Naomi, or Orpah.

_____ 1. There was a joyful reunion when I arrived back home in Moab.

_____ 2. I have a great fondness for my mother-in-law.

_____ 3. I was unlucky enough to be widowed.

_____ 4. Right now, I feel that I am "bad luck."

_____ 5. She is a very obedient and hard working girl.

_____ 6. I never expected anyone to take any interest in me because I was a foreigner.

_____ 7. I first saw Ruth when she was gathering grain.

_____ 8. I worried that some harm might come to Ruth.

_____ 9. I believe one of my greatest talents is being a matchmaker.

_____ 10. I think of her as my own daughter.

_____ 11. I had a lot of faith in Boaz's honor and responsibility.

_____ 12. I never regretted making a new life in Israel with a new husband.

RUTH
Ruth 1:1—4:22

Directions: Define the following words as Ruth would have.

sorrow: kindness:

family: ingenuity:

loyalty: patience:

happiness: love:

PROMISED LAND
REVIEW: Who's Who

Directions: Identify the following people. Reread the Scripture quotes from Chapter 5 if you need help.

Deborah—   **Jael—**

Delilah—   **Joshua—**

Eglon—   **Manoah—**

Ehud—   **Rahab—**

Gideon—   **Samson—**

Jabin—   **Sisera—**

PROMISED LAND
REVIEW: Bible Game

Activity 15

Directions: Place one of the names below in each of the boxes. The names do not have to follow the same order and only sixteen of the eighteen will be used. Do not repeat any name. Wait for further directions from the teacher.

Joash

Joshua

Rahab

Ehud

Eglon

Samson's father

Deborah

Jabin

Sisera

Barak

Jael

Gideon

Manoah

Samson

Delilah

Dagon

Purah

Samson's wife

Baal

Early Nationalism

ISRAEL'S FIRST KING
1 Samuel 9:1-27, 10:1-27, 11:1-15

Activity 1

Directions: Below is a character wheel for Saul. Each spoke of the wheel represents some fact or personality trait you have learned about Saul. Fill in the spokes of the wheel.

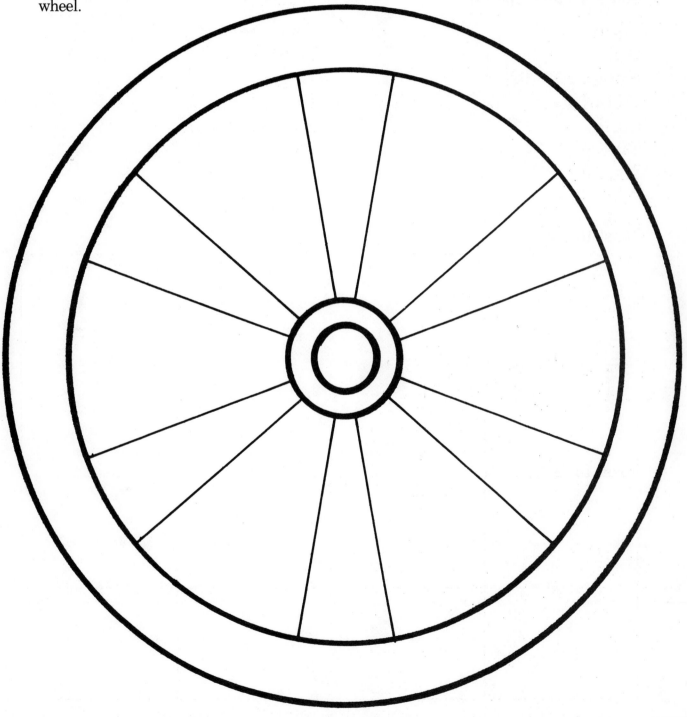

ISRAEL'S FIRST KING

Activity 2

1 Samuel 9:1-27, 10:1-27, 11:1-15

Directions: You have been asked, as Saul's speech writer, to prepare his speech for the banquet following the victorious battle with the Ammonites. As a shrewd politician, you can leave nothing to chance, so you also write "impromptu" toasts that will be offered to Saul by loyal supporters.

Saul's Victory Speech

Toast to Saul

Toast to Saul

DAVID AND GOLIATH

Activity 3

1 Samuel 17:1-58, 18:1-5

Directions: Which props go with which character? Place the correct numbers above the drawing of the character. Some items may be used more than once.

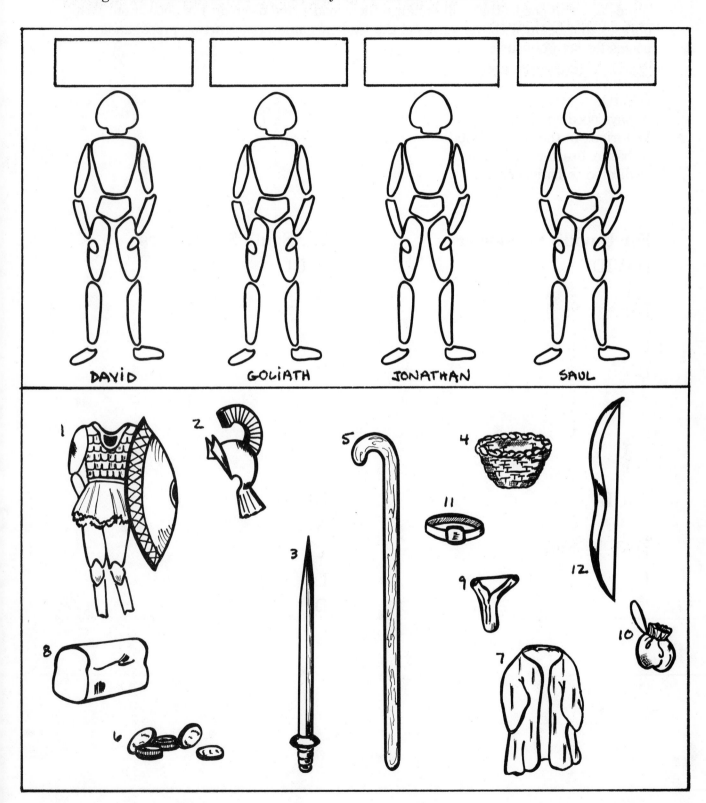

DAVID AND GOLIATH

1 Samuel 17:1-58, 18:1-5

Directions: Following the fight with Goliath, a new faction arose in Israel, one that supported David rather than Saul. You are the poet who has been commissioned by *both* camps to write poems that will enhance their leader and discredit the opposition. Write phrases that begin with the letters of the leaders' names, constructing propaganda poems for both of your clients.

Example:
DAVID
Always obedient son,
Victorious in the name of God,
In battle, greater than Saul,
Dedicated to Israel's cause.

For David's Supporters:

DAVID

A

V

I

D

For Saul's Supporters:

SAUL

A

U

L

SAUL

A

U

L

DAVID

A

V

I

D

SAUL'S REIGN

1 Samuel 18:6-30, 19:1-18, 28:3-25, 31:1-13

Directions: Upon Saul's death, the Philistines have decided to mock Israel by writing a history of her disreputable king. The Philistines do not have to invent stories, for Saul's life provides many examples of infamy. You are to choose five scenes for the book and justify your choices to the editor.

Scene 1
Justification:

Scene 2
Justification:

Scene 3
Justification:

Scene 4
Justification:

Scene 5
Justification:

SAUL'S REIGN

1 Samuel 18:6-30, 19:1-18, 28:3-25, 31:1-13

Directions: Design a record cover and album title that illustrate the main happenings of this section. Then make up six song titles that would be appropriate in this album. An example for a song title is "Suspicion," which describes one of Saul's feelings about David.

Side One	**Side Two**
1. Suspicion	1.
2.	2.
3.	3.
4.	

DAVID AND BATHSHEBA   Activity 7

2 Samuel 11:1-27, 12:1-25

Directions: After reading the passage, explain what comes to your mind when you see the following words.

City gate:

Wine:

Letter:

Mourning:

Lamb:

Rooftop:

Fasting:

Arrows:

Judgement:

Death:

DAVID AND BATHSHEBA

Activity 8

2 Samuel 11:1-27, 12:1-25

Directions: Choose the *real* David from your choice of David 1, David 2, and David 3. Circle all *false* answers. Which David always answers correctly?

I. How would you describe Bathsheba?
David 1 She was Uriah's wife.
David 2 She was very beautiful.
David 3 I sent a messenger to get her and bring her to me.

II. Why did you send for Uriah?
David 1 I was worried because Bathsheba was pregnant and Uriah couldn't have been the father.
David 2 I wanted Uriah to come home to sleep with his wife.
David 3 I wanted to give Uriah a break from the battle.

III. What did Uriah do that didn't please you?
David 1 He slept at the Palace Gate.
David 2 He didn't go home to Bathsheba.
David 3 He told me it wouldn't be fair to go home to celebrate.

IV. When Uriah foiled your first plan, what did you do?
David 1 I wrote a letter to Joab.
David 2 I planned to make Uriah die an "accidental" death.
David 3 I invited him to supper and got him drunk.

V. What happened after Uriah's death?
David 1 Bathsheba mourned Uriah.
David 2 Bathsheba married me.
David 3 Bathsheba bore a son.

VI. Who was Nathan?
David 1 He was a prophet.
David 2 He told me a parable about a poor man and a rich man.
David 3 He told me all my children would die.

VII. What happened after your son became ill?
David 1 God was merciful and spared the child.
David 2 I wept and fasted.
David 3 He died.

VIII. What happened after your son died?
David 1 The Lord spoke to me and told me to name my next son Jedediah.
David 2 Solomon was born.
David 3 I broke my fast.

The "real David" is David #____

ABSALOM'S UPRISING

Activity 9

2 Samuel 15:1-16, 18:1-33

Directions: Listed below are factual statements, comprehension statements and synthesis statements. Respond to each statement by indicating whether you think the statement is true or false. Be ready to justify your answers.

I. Factual Statements

____ 1. Absalom won the loyalty of the Israelites.

____ 2. Absalom planned a rebellion against his father.

____ 3. The king escaped with his family from Jerusalem.

____ 4. David accompanied his troops.

____ 5. David's men defeated the Israelites.

____ 6. David ordered that Absalom be killed.

____ 7. David believed the messengers were bringing good news.

II. Comprehension Statements

____ 8. Absalom was a bad son.

____ 9. David loved Absalom.

____ 10. Absalom got what he deserved.

____ 11. Nathan's prophecy came true. (see 2 Samuel 12:1-25)

III. Synthesis Statements

____ 12. Parents love their children no matter what they do.

____ 13. Sometimes people enjoy bringing bad news.

____ 14. In a war, the soldiers should always obey their superior officers.

____ 15. Traitors to our country deserve to die.

ABSALOM'S UPRISING

Activity 10

2 Samuel 15:1-16, 18:1-33

Directions: A movie studio is doing a modern version of Absalom's story. As the director, make the following choices.
Which actors would you choose for the following roles? Also, explain why these actors would be most appropriate.

Absalom:
Explanation:

David:
Explanation:

Joab:
Explanation:

Ahimaaz:
Explanation:

David's man who found Absalom in the tree:
Explanation:

Where would you film each of these scenes?
2 Samuel 15:1-6
2 Samuel 18:1-5
2 Samuel 18:6-18
2 Samuel 18:24-33

What props would you use in each of the scenes?
2 Samuel 15:1-6
2 Samuel 18:1-5
2 Samuel 18:6-18
2 Samuel 18:24-33

PSALMS OF DAVID Activity 11

Psalm 23, 29

Directions: Fill in the blanks below to form words that are important to the main ideas of the two psalms. Explain the importance of each. Then summarize each Psalm's meaning.

Psalm 23

S _ E _ _ _ R _

_ E _ T

_ T _ E _ GT _

_ O _

_ _ _ FF

E _ E _ _ E _

_ _ P

_ OV _

Summary of Psalm 23:

Psalm 29

_ O _ ER

_ OI _ _

S _ _ S

_ _ U _ T _ I _ S

_ _ G _ _ NI _ _

K _ N _

_ EA _ _

Summary of Psalm 29:

PSALMS OF DAVID

Psalms 23, 29

Activity 12

Directions: Choose either Psalm 23 or 29 and illustrate for a child's book. Each square below should contain a drawing with an explanation.

The Lord is my shepherd

96

SOLOMON'S WISDOM

1 Kings 2:1-4, 3:1-28 Ecclesiastes 3:1-15

Directions: Before reading the selection above record what you would request if you could have one wish. Answer the additional questions about your wish.

MY WISH

1. Why did you select this particular wish?

2. Whom would benefit most from your wish?

Now read the selections from 1 Kings.
3. What did Solomon wish for?

4. How did God feel about his wish?

5. Compare your wish and Solomon's.

SOLOMON'S WISDOM

Activity 14

1 Kings 2:1-4, 3:1-28 Ecclesiastes 3:1-15

Directions: From magazines choose pictures that represent the important events in your life. Paste them in a collage on the page.

PROVERBS

Proverbs 10:1, 10:7, 10:12, 10:15, 10:20, 11:29, 13:7, 13:16, 15:1, 16:32

Directions: Complete each sentence according to the selection. Then write an original proverb, or wise saying.

Example: Biblical
A wise son *makes his father proud.*
Original
Wise children *do not try their parents' patience.*

Biblical—Proverbs 10:7
Good people_____
Original
Good people_____

Biblical—Proverbs 10:12
Love_____
Original
Love_____

Biblical—Proverbs 10:15
Poverty_____
Original
Poverty_____

Biblical—Proverbs 10:20
The words of a good man_____
Original
The words of a good person_____

Biblical—Proverbs 11:29
A fool_____
Original
A fool_____

Biblical—Proverbs 13:17

People who pretend to be rich_____

Original

People who pretend to be rich_____

Biblical—Proverbs 13:16

Sensible people_____

Original

Sensible people_____

Biblical—Proverbs 15:1

A quiet answer_____

Original

A quiet answer_____

Biblical—Proverbs 16:32

Patience_____

Original

Patience_____

PROVERBS

Proverbs 10:1, 10:7, 10:12, 10:15, 10:20, 11:29, 13:7, 13:16, 15:1, 16:32

Directions: Make a poster illustrating either a Biblical proverb or one of your own.

TRIBULATIONS OF JOB   Activity 17

Job 1:1—2:13, 4:1-11, 12:1-3, 13:22-28, 38:1-18, 42:1-17

Directions: Select a modern counterpart to Job, before he was afflicted with trials.

Describe:
1. his job
2. his office
3. his hobbies
4. his house
5. his cars
6. his best friend
7. his children
8. his ambition
9. his political connections
10. his daily newspaper
11. his most often read book
12. his favorite restaurant

TRIBULATIONS OF JOB

Activity 18

Job 1:1—2:13, 4:1-11, 12:1-3, 13:22-28, 38:1-18, 42:1-17

Directions: Write possible inscriptions on the tombstones.

Here lies
Job's Wife

Here lies
Job

Here lies
Job's Oldest Son

EARLY NATIONALISM
REVIEW: Who's Who

Directions: Identify the following people. Reread Scripture quotes of Chapter 6 if you need help.

Absalom—

Bathsheba—

David—

Eliphaz—

Goliath—

Joab—

Job—

Jonathon—

Michal—

Nathan—

Samuel—

Saul—

Solomon—

Uriah—

Copyright © 1984, Winston Press, Inc.

EARLY NATIONALISM
REVIEW: Crossword Game   Activity 20

Directions: Complete the following crossword with names and objects found in the unit. Scrambled words are found vertically below each column.

```
T  R  S  H  I  N  H  U  H  D  T  D  A  O  O  M  Y  A
      A  E  E  P  G  L  M  I  B  S  A  L  K  R     L
      P  L  L     U  A  M  V  C  H  O  L  O  E     U
      S  E  O     L  E  R  N     A  R  O  O        S
      S           A  S     O     A  B  N           S
      R           E  M     A     B  B  S
                             W   R  Y  O
                             I      Y  M
                             D
                             W
```

Prophetic Messages

ELIJAH
1 Kings 16:29-34, 17:1-24, 18:1-46

Activity 1

Directions: List the important steps Elijah took to relieve the drought by labeling each rung on the ladder with important words or deeds. Be ready to explain your answers.

ELIJAH

1 Kings 16:29-34, 17:1-24, 18:1-46

Directions: Assume that you can go back in time to the competition of Elijah and the prophets of Baal. Tension is mounting while the crowd gathers before the great event. As a sportscaster, you are to interview the participants and key observers.

Questions asked of Elijah:

    Elijah's response:

Questions asked of Ahab:

    Ahab's response:

Questions asked of Obadiah:

    Obadiah's response:

Questions asked of Jezebel:

    Jezebel's response:

Questions asked of Baal's prophet:

    Response of Baal's prophet:

SELECTION OF JEREMIAH　　Activity 3

Jeremiah 1:1-19, 2:1-19

Directions: From God's point of view, write an adjective for each letter of the alphabet describing the nation of Israel. Be able to explain why each applies.

A _____

B _____

C _____

D _____

E _____

F _____

G _____

H _____

I _____

J _____

K _____

L _____

M _____

N _____

O _____

P _____

Q _____

R _____

S _____

T _____

U _____

V _____

W _____

X, Y, Z _____

SELECTION OF JEREMIAH Activity 4

Jeremiah 1:1-19, 2:1-19

Directions: Write a form poem or tanka, describing God's feelings toward Israel. Use the correct number of syllables per line. Do not rhyme the lines of the poem.

_____ (five syllables)

_____ (seven syllables)

_____ (five syllables)

_____ (seven syllables)

_____ (seven syllables)

JEREMIAH'S DEPRESSION Activity 5

Jeremiah 20:7-18

Directions: Before reading Jeremiah 20:7-18, make a list of causes of frustration to you.

Using a scale of 5 (1 = minor frustrations, 5 = extreme frustration), rate the items in the boxes to the left.

Read Jeremiah 20:7-18. Compile a list of Jeremiah's extreme frustrations.

JEREMIAH'S DEPRESSION Activity 6

Jeremiah 20:7-18

Directions: Design a greeting card that a friend might have sent to Jeremiah.

OUTSIDE

INSIDE

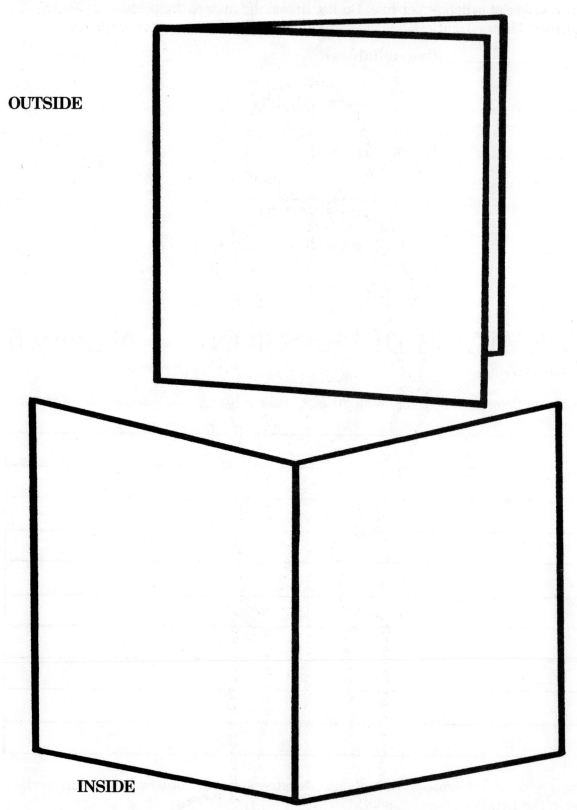

JONAH

Jonah 1:1—4:11

Directions: Jonah is divided in half. On the left draw anything that relates to Jonah's disobedience. On the right side portray anything that relates to Jonah's obedience.

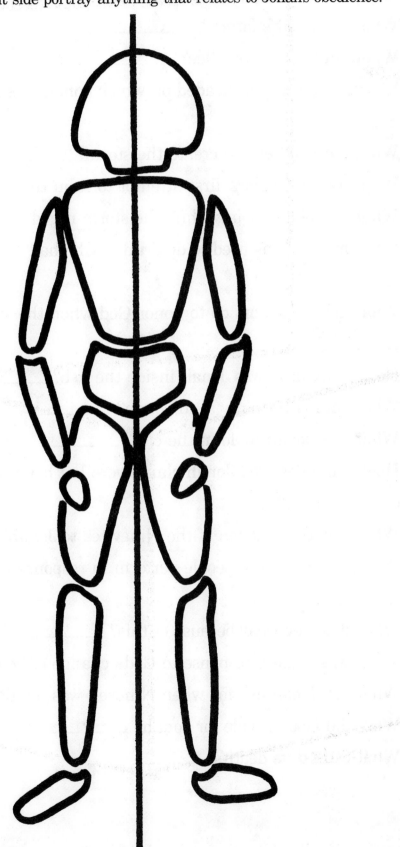

JONAH

Jonah 1:1—4:11

Directions: After reading the questions below, find the correct answers below. Place the appropriate *letter* in the space provided. (Letters may be used more than once.)

1. Who was Jonah's father? _____

2. Where did Jonah first flee? _____

3. Where was the ship headed on which Jonah was a passenger?

    _____

4. What did God send to create the storm? _____

5. What was the sailors' first attempt to calm the storm? _____

6. What was Jonah doing while the storm raged? _____

7. What method was used to determine who had caused the storm?

    _____

8. What did the sailors do to honor God when the storm stopped?

    _____

9. How many days was Jonah inside the fish? _____

10. Where did God finally send Jonah? _____

11. What was Jonah to do in the city? _____

12. How many days did Jonah claim were left before Nineveh's

    destruction? _____

13. What was the reaction of the Ninevites to Jonah's message? _____

14. What action did the people perform in response to Jonah's message?

    _____

15. What did they wear because of this? _____

16. What was Jonah's response to God's change of heart? _____

17. What did Jonah ask for when Nineveh was not destroyed? _____

18. What did God provide for Jonah? _____

19. What caused its death? _____

20. What was Jonah's response to this? _____

21. God told Jonah that there were 120,000 children in which city?

_____

22. Because of what other occupants of the city did God pity Nineveh?

_____

Answers:

A. worm
B. Nineveh
C. anger
D. three
E. wind
F. sackcloth
G. forty

H. death
I. Tarshish (Spain)
J. cattle
K. casting lots
L. repentance
M. sleeping
N. sacrifice

O. plant
P. Joppa
Q. fasting
R. Amittai
S. preach
T. prayer

Directions: Now that you have found the answers to the questions, connect the lettered dots starting with your first answer and proceeding through answer 22. (Some dots will be connected more than once.) When you are finished, you should see a picture that relates to the selection you have read.

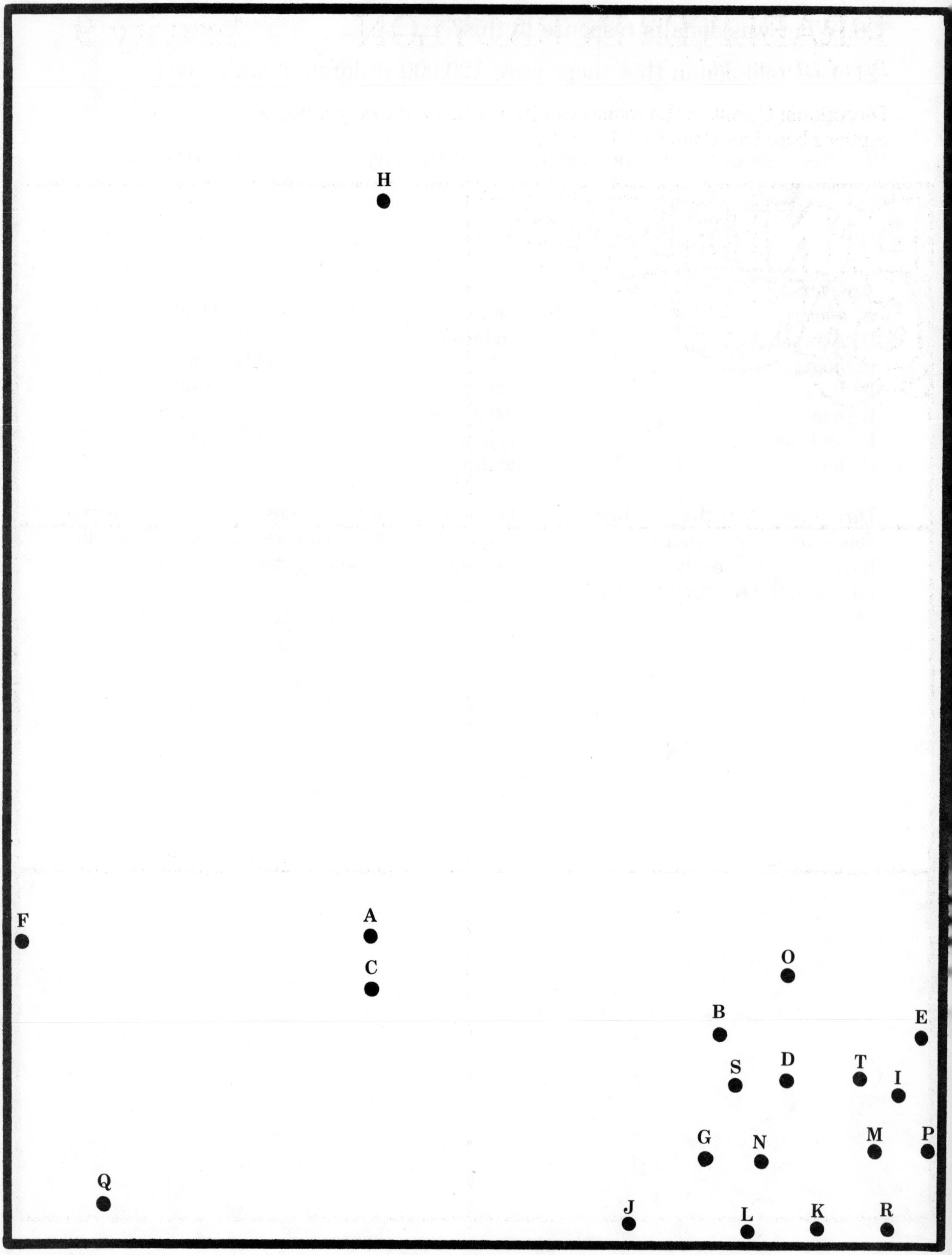

H

F

A

C

O

B

E

S

D

T

I

G

N

M

P

Q

J

L

K

R

ISRAELITES IN BABYLON   Activity 9

Daniel 1:1-7, 3:1-30

Directions: Complete the comic strip frames below drawing pictures and writing captions based on Daniel 1:1-7, 3:1-30.

DANIEL'S GANG

ISRAELITES IN BABYLON   Activity 10

Daniel 1:1-7, 3:1-30

Directions: Complete the sentences below as you feel the characters would.

Nebuchadnezzar

1. I admire _____.

2. I command _____.

3. I dislike _____.

4. I fear _____.

5. I worship _____.

6. I regret _____.

7. I believe _____.

8. I promote _____.

Daniel's three friends

1. We refuse _____.

2. We fear _____.

3. We honor _____.

4. We dislike _____.

5. We obey _____.

6. We trust _____.

7. We risk _____.

DANIEL

Daniel 5:1-31, 6:1-28

Directions: Give an example of how Daniel fits each of the following roles.

1. leader

2. rebel

3. hero

4. friend

5. servant

6. prophet

7. victim

8. holy man

9. exile

DANIEL

Daniel 5:1-31, 6:1-28

Activity 12

Directions: King Darius is planning an awards banquet. You have been asked to design and inscribe a plaque to be presented to Daniel. The design should be tasteful and the inscription indicative of the King's admiration for Daniel.

ISAIAH

Isaiah 2:1-5, 9:1-7, 11:1-9, 35:1-10

Directions: Write a commemoration to peace by completing each of the lines. Rhymes are not necessary.

Peace is _____

Peace is _____

Peace is _____

Peace is _____

Peace is _____

Peace is _____

Peace is _____

Peace is _____

(Complete with a final statement)

_____

ISAIAH

Isaiah 2:1-5, 9:1-7, 11:1-9, 35:1-10

Directions: Each word below has something to do with the selection you have read from Isaiah. Classify each word as having either a good (+) or bad (−) connotation. Then, explain how each word relates to this selection.

darkness, harvest, yoke, child, peace, battle, wisdom, reverence, singing, lions, fools, desert, dance, rescue, afraid, tired

+

1. :_____

2. :_____

3. :_____

4. :_____

5. :_____

6. :_____

7. :_____

8. :_____

—

1. :_____

2. :_____

3. :_____

4. :_____

5. :_____

6. :_____

7. :_____

8. :_____

Copyright © 1984, Winston Press, Inc.

PROPHETIC MESSAGES
REVIEW: Who's Who   Activity 15

Directions: Identify the following people. Reread Scripture quotes of Chapter 7 if you need help.

Abednego—

Ahab—

Belshazzar—

Daniel—

Darius—

Elijah—

Isaiah—

Jeremiah—

Jezebel—

Jonah—

Meshach—

Nebuchadnezzar—

Shadrach—

PROPHETIC MESSAGES
REVIEW: Game

Directions: It is your job to decipher the message in code. Each letter has been assigned a number. You have been given three clues to help you break the code: **3 = T, 14 = H,** and **25 = E.** Go through the puzzle and put a T in the blanks with a 3 beneath, etc. Fill in the puzzle by discovering the new letters. This puzzle will tell you something about the unit you just finished.

T	H	E											
3	14	25	20	8	11	20	14	25	3	24	15	4	15

19	16	10	13	16	19	16	9	4	10	26

3	14	4	10	26	24 :	18	8	11	23	26	14	3

16	7	14	4	6	15	18	16	7	5	3	11

6	4	2	25 ,	7	16	6	6	25	15

15	11	1	10	2	4	8	25	2	8	11	19

14	25	16	22	25	10 ,	24	3	16	13	25	15

16	6	4	22	25	4	10	16	2	4	24	14 ,

16	10	15	24	23	8	22	4	22	25	15	16

,							
6	4	11	10	24	15	25	10 .

Jesus

JESUS' BIRTH
Luke 1:26-38, 2:1-20 Matthew 2:1-12

Directions: Each of the items below is important to the story of Jesus' birth. Choose five persons or objects from the list and design a concrete poem for each. To design a concrete poem, imagine characteristics of the person or object being illustrated then use the letters of the word to make a design that reflects those characteristics.

Example:

ANGEL	**SHEPHERD**	**MARY**
CENSUS	**KINGS** (or wise men)	**JOSEPH**
BABY	**HEROD**	**STAR**
MANGER	**JESUS**	**BETHLEHEM**
INN	**DECREE**	

JESUS' BIRTH

Activity 2

Luke 1:26-38, 2:1-20 Matthew 2:1-12

Directions: Use prepositions from the list to write cumulative sentences that reflect an idea from the above Scripture selections. You may not use prepositional phrases directly from the selection.

at	of	between
by	for	behind
in	with	below
on	like	beneath
near	about	beside
to	above	before
from	across	beyond
down	after	despite
off	against	during
through	along	except
out	amid	toward
past	among	under
up	amount	

BAPTISM AND TEMPTATION   Activity 3

Matthew 3:1-17, 4:1-11

Directions: Study the answers below. Fill in the questions that would prompt these answers.

Example: Question: What did John do?
                 Answer: Baptize

1. **Question:**

   Answer: John the Baptist

2. **Question:**

   Answer: water

3. **Question:**

   Answer: camel's hair

4. **Question:**

   Answer: "This is my son, with whom I am well pleased."

5. **Question:**

   Answer: dove

6. **Question:**

   Answer: leather

7. **Question:**

   Answer: the temple

8. **Question:**

   Answer: Pharisees

9. **Question:**

   Answer: locusts

10. **Question:**

    Answer: forty days and nights

BAPTISM AND TEMPTATION   Activity 4

Matthew 3:1-17, 4:1-11

Directions: Read the verse and fill in the chart below by completing Jesus' responses to the devil's temptations. In the second chart, record several instances in which you have been tempted to commit an unwise or immoral act.

Temptations	Jesus' Responses
1. Turn the stones into bread.	1.
2. Throw yourself down from the highest point of the Temple.	2.
3. Receive all the world's kingdoms for worship of the devil.	3.

Your Temptations	Your Responses
1.	1.
2.	2.
3.	3.
4.	4.

THE DISCIPLES AND THE SERMON ON THE MOUNT

Activity 5

Matthew 4:18-25, 5:1-16

Directions: Write Simon's (Peter's), Andrew's, James' or John's diary describing personal feelings about becoming Jesus' disciple.

What would your reactions be if Jesus came and asked you to be his disciple and to leave your family and possessions behind? Fill in your own diary selection below.

Dear Diary,

Signed,

THE DISCIPLES AND THE SERMON ON THE MOUNT

Activity 6

Matthew 4:18-25, 5:1-16

Directions: Before reading Matthew 4:18-25, 5:1-16, what, in your opinion, makes people happy? Fill in the blanks below.

1. Happy are those who _____

2. Happy are those who _____

3. Happy are those who _____

4. Happy are those who _____

5. Happy are those who _____

6. Happy are those who _____

7. Happy are those who _____

8. Happy are those who _____

9. Happy are those who _____

After reading the passage, complete the sentences according to Matthew 4:18-25, 5:1-16.

1. Happy are those who _____

2. Happy are those who _____

3. Happy are those who _____

4. Happy are those who _____

5. Happy are those who _____

6. Happy are those who _____

7. Happy are those who _____

8. Happy are those who _____

9. Happy are those who _____

PARABLES

Luke 13:18-21, 15:1-32

Activity 7

Directions: Read the suggested verses and try to analyze some of the comparisons that are made by answering the questions below.

1. How is God's kingdom like a mustard seed? List three qualities that they have in common.

    a.

    b.

    c.

2. How is God's kingdom like making bread? List three qualities that they have in common.

    a.

    b.

    c.

3. Make your own comparisons to God's kingdom and list common qualities.

    A. God's kingdom is like_____.

    　　1.

    　　2.

    　　3.

    B. God's kingdom is like _____.

    　　1.

    　　2.

    　　3.

    C. God's kingdom is like _____.

    　　1.

    　　2.

    　　3.

PARABLES

Luke 13:18-21

Directions: Make up slogan buttons for the father, the older son and the younger son. Decorate them.

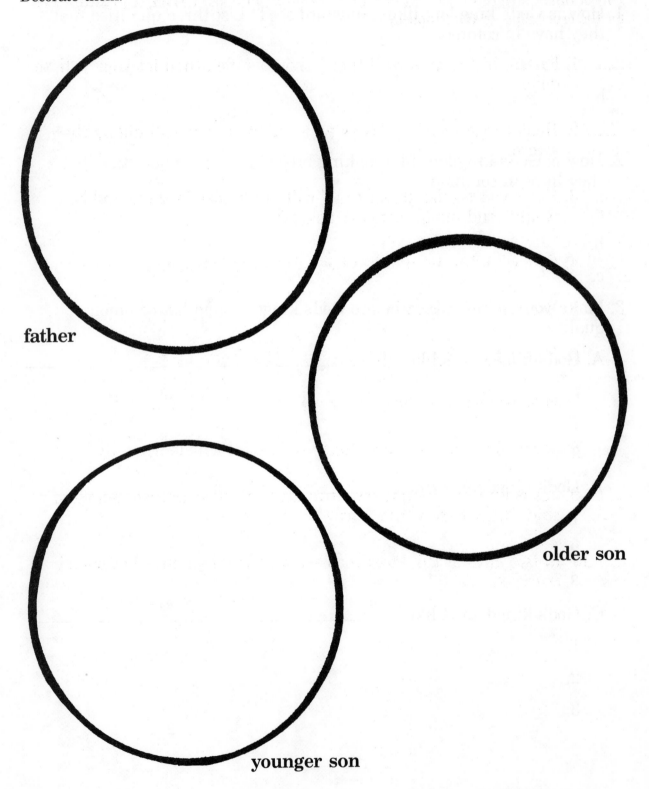

father

older son

younger son

ENTRY INTO JERUSALEM AND ARREST

Activity 9

Matthew 21:1-17, 26:1-56

Directions: Categorize each statement as: (**A**) Jesus' faith, (**B**) Lesson, (**C**) Preparations for the crucifixion, or (**D**) Prophecy.

_____ 1. Father, if it is your will that I should suffer, then let your will be done.

_____ 2. Replace your sword. Those who use the sword will die by the sword.

_____ 3. Don't you realize that I could call my Father for help and he would send me an army of angels?

_____ 4. One who dips bread with me will be my betrayer.

_____ 5. You will abandon me.

_____ 6. Before the rooster crows you will deny knowing me.

_____ 7. Poor people will always be with you but I will not.

_____ 8. Jesus gave the disciples bread and said, "This is my body."

_____ 9. Jesus and his disciples went to a place called Gethsemane and said, "Stay here while I pray."

_____ 10. In two days at the Passover Festival I will be handed over and crucified.

ENTRY INTO JERUSALEM AND ARREST   Activity 10

Matthew 21:1-17, 26:1-56

Directions: You have been commissioned by a church to design six stained glass windows. Make six preliminary sketches, representing each group of verses.

Example:

Matthew 26:36-46

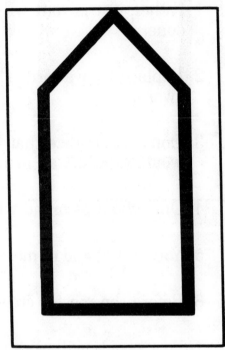

Matthew 21:1-11

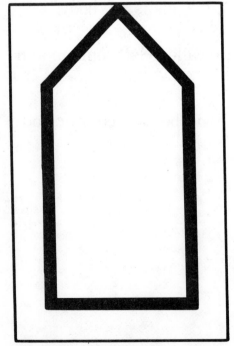

Matthew 21:12-17

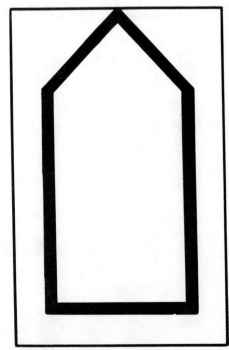

Matthew 26:17-35

Matthew 26:36-46

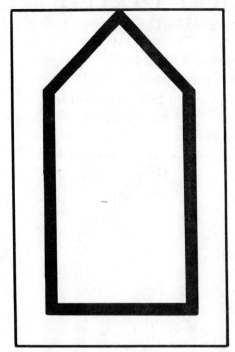

Matthew 26:47-56

JESUS' DEATH

Matthew 26:57—27:56

Activity 11

Directions: Write descriptive words for the people in the scenes. Beside each description include a quote to illustrate it.

Peter (Simon)

1.

2.

Judas

1.

2.

Pilate

1.

2.

Soldiers

1.

2.

Jesus

1.

2.

3.

4.

JESUS' DEATH

Activity 12

Matthew 26:57—27:56

Directions: Unscramble the key words below. Each word has something to do with an action or an idea in the reading. Explain why these words are important to the passage. (Some of the words may be found exactly in your selection and some may be synonyms for words in the selection.)

1. srerat

2. salef decenvie

3. neyd

4. roteros

5. yhritt vilres onics

6. oldbo nemyo

7. tarew

8. nowrc fo shontr

9. niew

10. theolcs

11. peltem

12. icyfruc

13. rkenasds

14. keatquraeh

BURIAL AND RESURRECTION

Activity 13

Matthew 27:57—28:20

Directions: Assume that you are a follower of Jesus and are present at the crucifixion. Leaving Golgotha, you hear the comments of bystanders and speak with some of the disciples. Record their possible reactions.

*Pharisee:

Mary Magdalene:

Peter:

Young woman:

Old man:

Soldier:

Joseph of Arimathea:

*Legalistic Jewish sect, accused by Jesus of being hypocrites (see Luke 11:37-44).

BURIAL AND RESURRECTION

Matthew 27:57—28:20

Directions: Following is a list of outline headings and subheadings. Find the five main headings printed in capital letters and put them in chronological order, starting with **I** and ending with **V**. Then, group the remaining headings under the correct main headings. Finally, give the whole selection a title.

Title

I.

    A.

    B.

II.

    A.

    B.

III.

    A.

    B.

    C.

    D.

    E.

IV.

    A.

    B.

V.

    A.

    B.

Some disciples doubted

A RICH MAN BURIED JESUS

Body wrapped in linen

Jesus clothed in white

Priests gave soldiers money

GUARDS INFORMED CHIEF PRIESTS OF RESURRECTION

Guards implicated disciples in alleged theft of body

Body placed in tomb

GUARDS AT JESUS' TOMB

Jesus ordered disciples to find more disciples

DISCIPLES SAW JESUS RESURRECTED

Chief priests and Pharisees met with Pilate

Put seal on tomb

Earthquake rocked area

JESUS' RESURRECTION

Women filled with joy

Angel spoke to women

Guards fearful

138

LOVE

I Corinthians 13:1-13

Directions: Find pictures to illustrate the following.

Characteristics of Love	Characteristics Not Associated With Love
patience	arrogance
kindness	selfishness
truthful	jealousy
eternal	ill-mannered
hope	vengeful

LOVE

I Corinthians 13:1-13

Directions: Although modern newspapers generally describe acts of hatred, read a newspaper looking for acts of love. Clip the headlines and place them in the gift boxes below.

NEW HEAVEN AND EARTH   Activity 17

Revelation 6:1-17, 20:11-15, 21:1-7

Directions: Define each of the following modern values. Explain how each could lead to the destruction of the world as we know it.

power—

money—

beauty—

satisfaction—

knowledge—

curiosity—

personal accomplishment—

love—

security—

pride—

NEW HEAVEN AND EARTH   Activity 18
Revelation 6:1-17, 20:11-15, 21:1-7

Directions: Before reading the above Scripture selection, choose the color that you most closely associate with the object listed below. Place the letter of the color in the correct space at the left of the object.

A. white   **B.** red   **C.** black   **D.** pale

____ 1. sword

____ 2. victorious king

____ 3. starving child

____ 4. bombed building

____ 5. polio

____ 6. sun

____ 7. earthquake

____ 8. parade of conquerors

____ 9. heart attack·

____ 10. tornado

____ 11. drought

____ 12. nuclear war

____ 13. defeated city

____ 14. locusts

____ 15. corpse

____ 16. poison

____ 17. flood

____ 18. decorated soldier

____ 19. overpopulation

____ 20. cancer

Now read Revelation 6:1-17, 20:11-15, 21:1-7. From this vision of the end of the world, explain what each of the above colors do represent. How similar were your color associations?

White:

Red:

Black:

Pale:

THE LIFE OF JESUS
REVIEW: Who's Who

Directions: Identify the following people.

Andrew—

Barabbas—

Caiaphas—

Gabriel—

Herod—

James—

John—

John the Baptist—

Joseph—

Joseph of Arimathea—

Judas Iscariot—

Mary—

Mary Magdalene—

Peter (Simon)—

Pilate—

Prodigal Son—

JESUS REVIEW:
Word Scramble

Activity 20

Directions: Unscramble the words below. Consider people, places, and things associated with Jesus' life. Unscramble the circled letters to decode the secret message below.

1. T L B E E M H E H

2. B E A R L P A

3. O C W R N   F O   H N S R O T

4. R T E E P

5. E P L M E T

6. N H J O   H E T   T P B I T S A

7. H M E A N G E T S E

8. A A T R Z E N H

9. I A E T P L

10. C P E I I S S D L

Message:

Resources

Beginnings Unit

Activity 1
An example is provided for day number one. Brainstorming for ideas is a profitable starting point.

Activity 2
As the students write pattern poems, encourage them to choose words that are not in the text, thereby making the exercise as creative as possible. Poems can be read aloud or placed on colored paper, surrounded by magazine clippings to illustrate them.

Example:
line 1: God
line 2: powerful, wonderful
line 3: existing, molding, organizing
line 4: transformed the awesome void
line 5: creator

Activity 3
Among the qualities students might list for Eden are immortality, innocence, closeness to God, and lack of pain. Ask them to compare or contrast their concepts of Eden and our society. The purpose is to compare our society with a utopia.

Activity 4
The intent of this exercise is to suggest that the Bible be read with new perspective. Adam and Eve are not stock characters, precursors of the human race. Rather, they are presented as people quite capable of emotion and surely surprised by new experiences.

Activity 5
Each apple represents evil or sin. Students should label the apples with words such as pride, envy, or shame. A discussion will establish students' perceptions of evil.

Activity 6

1
The snake was a most beguiling creature
(Genesis 3:1)

2
Eve told snake that they were forbidden to eat from tree
(Genesis 3:2-3)

3
Eve took some of the fruit, as did Adam
(Genesis 3:6)

4
Adam and Eve were embarrassed by their nakedness
(Genesis 3:7)

5
Adam and Eve hid from God
(Genesis 3:8)

6
Adam blamed Eve
(Genesis 3:12)

7
Snake was punished
(Genesis 3:14)

8
Adam's punishment was a life of hard work
(Genesis 3:17-19)

9
God placed flaming sword on east side of garden
(Genesis 3:24)

Activity 7
Answer Key:
1. True (Cain was older.)
2. True
3. False (Cain suggested that they go and no reason was given.)
4. False (The mark was to protect him.)
5. True
6. True
7. Not Mentioned
8. Not Mentioned
9. False (Abel's blood cried out to him from the ground.)
10. Not Mentioned
11. True
12. Not Mentioned

Activity 8
Students are to draw their answers in the appropriate squares of the personal shield. To the question, "What was Cain's position in his family?", students could draw a large number one.

Activity 9
The teacher may want to break the class into groups and assign each group a word ending. See how many words each group can think of to describe Noah. The words cannot be coined words. Students may complete their lists with words from other groups.

Activity 10
God's voice may be part of the dialogue to encourage a closer following of the text. The activity, on the other hand, may begin at the conclusion of God's promise to Noah in order to prompt a more inventive dialogue.

Activity 11
Activity 11 should be completed before reading Genesis 11:1-9

Etymology (the study of names and word origins) plays an important role in the first Biblical stories. The purpose of this activity is to understand etymology by considering common names and associated characteristics.

Finally, students should read Genesis 11:1-9 to discover how *Babel* received its name. Look for other examples of etymology while studying the Bible. So far, the names of *Eve* and *Cain* have both been mentioned in this context.

Activity 12
Monuments may be individual or group creations. They should represent good and bad aspects of society, or, in other words, our total society. A monument may be a configuration of a cross, to represent religion, and the dollar sign. Big cars or fancy clothes could also symbolize our society's materialism. Each monument should consist of numerous details. Students should be ready to discuss their monuments.

Activity 13
Answer Key:
Abel: second child of Adam and Eve; shepherd; pleased God; killed by Cain.
Adam: first human; made from the dust of the earth.
Cain: firstborn of Adam and Eve; farmer; killed his brother Abel; wanderer in a land east of Eden.
Eve: companion for Adam; made from one of Adam's ribs; disobeyed God's command; the name means mother of all human beings.
Ham: son of Noah; saved from the flood.
Japheth: son of Noah; saved from the flood.
Noah: chosen by God to escape the flood because of his righteousness.
Shem: son of Noah; saved from the flood.
Snake: tempted Eve to eat the fruit from the tree in the middle of the Garden of Eden; his punishment was to crawl on his belly.
Note: Adam's name in Hebrew means *mankind*.

Activity 14
Answer Key:

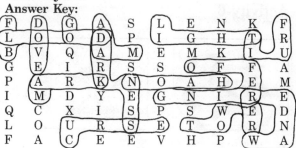

Patriarchs Unit

Activity 1
Answer Key:
1. Abram
2. Abram/Lot
3. Abram
4. Abram
5. Abram
6. Abram
7. Lot
8. Abram
9. Abram

Activity 2
Brief answers are acceptable; however, the teacher may divide the class into groups and assign each group one of the seven suggested changes for expanded story adaptations.

Activity 3

An example of a similarity is: Sarai/Hagar—treated each other spitefully at one time or another. An example of a difference is: Sarai/Hagar—Sarai was barren, but Hagar could have children. There should be no repetition of likenesses and differences. Difference in gender should not be allowed as an answer.

Activity 4

The first set of statements is to be considered before reading Genesis 16:1-15; the second set of statements is to be evaluated afterwards. Both are designed for discussion—the first for appraisal of the students' moral and social norms and the second for comparison between modern behavior and social conventions of Abram's time. In order to best compare the two time periods, consider statements 1 and 7 then statements 2 and 8. Similarly numbered statements deal with similar situations.

Activity 5

This activity tests the students' comprehension of the passage. The length of the blanks do not correlate to the length of the answers. Each blank represents one word.

Suggested answers:

Abraham was a very *hospitable* man. When he saw *travelers* passing by his *tent* he ran out to *greet* them and asked them to *stop* and *rest* while he *brought* *food* and *served* them. Sarah baked *bread*. Abraham ordered a *servant* to prepare a *fatted* *calf* for their *meal*. The strangers informed Abraham that Sarah would *have* *a* *child* in *nine* *months*, an announcement that *amused* the *couple* since Sarah was past the age of *child-bearing*. Sarah also felt *fear* at the announcement. The strangers must have been *angels*.

Then Abraham *accompanied* the strangers to a place where they could look down on *Sodom*. At this time the Lord decided to take *Abraham* into his confidence. The Lord told *Abraham* that the people of Sodom and *Gomorrah* were *sinful* and that He planned to *destroy* the towns. Abraham felt *sad* at the news and *questioned* the Lord. Abraham was *bold* to speak to the Lord and ask questions in regard to Sodom and Gomorrah.

Lot, like *Abraham*, offered to serve the *strangers* who came to town. They went with Lot to his *house*. The men of Sodom made *wicked* advances and Lot *begged* them not to be so *wicked*. All the men who came to Lot's house were made *blind*. Lot was *advised* by the *angels* to leave Sodom. So Lot *gathered* his family together in order to *flee*. Lot was *hesitant* to leave, but the Lord felt *pity* and *spared* him. Lot was probably spared because of his *generosity*. The *strangers* ordered the family not to look back. Lot's wife, a very *anxious* woman, did look back and was turned into a *pillar* *of* *salt*. The next day Sodom and Gomorrah were only *ashes* in the desert.

Activity 6

The headlines should introduce the following stories: SKY RAINS FIRE: Destruction of Sodom and Gomorrah. GUESTS FIND TOWN FAR FROM HOSPITABLE: Angels visit Sodom.

ABRAHAM BARTERS WITH GOD: God promises Abraham not to destroy Sodom if ten innocent people can be found. NEW MONUMENT TO BE DEDICATED IN DESERT: Lot's wife is turned into a pillar of salt when she looks back at the destruction of Sodom and Gomorrah.

Encourage students to elaborate, furnishing details not necessarily included in the text.

Note: God has changed Abram's name to Abraham and Sarai's name to Sarah (Genesis 17:1-15).

Activity 7
Answer Key:

1.	C	7.	I
2.	E	8.	J
3.	F	9.	A
4.	G	10.	B
5.	H	11.	L
6.	D	12.	K

Activity 8

The Biblical story of Abraham only hints at conflicts between husband and wife, wife and concubine, father and son. In order to better understand family relationships, students should complete one or more interview forms. The class can be divided into the four character groups and answer the questions in this manner. In this case, a volunteer can take the role of interviewer and pose the questions to the groups' spokesmen.

Activity 9

In this exercise students are asked to determine how characters felt about each other. In some instances the verses tell exactly how characters felt; in other cases the student is asked to read between the lines. For instance, in 2 Jacob is his mother's favorite; in 4 Esau is Isaac's favorite.

Activity 10

To compare and contrast is the main thrust of this activity. The overlapping area of the two circles should contain characteristics or deeds the characters have in common. The rest of the circles should contain characteristics or deeds that the characters do not share.

Activity 11

Students should read the selection and determine qualities or characteristics of Laban and Jacob. For instance, Laban's asking the shepherds for information shows that he is *seeking*. Jacob is described as being *prosperous*. Compare answers.

Activity 12

Activity 12 should be finished before reading Genesis 29:1-30. It sets the tone for a discussion about deceit (misleading a person through trickery). This is significant because there are many deceptive schemes in the Jacob narrative.

Deceptions found in Genesis 25:19-34, 27:1-45: Rebecca and Jacob tricked Isaac into giving Jacob the blessing of the first born. Rebecca tricked Esau by sending Jacob to Laban.

Deceptions found in Genesis 29:1-30: Laban tricked Jacob by substituting Leah for Rachel at their wedding.

Deceptions found in Genesis 30:25-43, 31:1-3, 31:17-21, 33:18-20: Jacob tricked Laban by placing spotted branches in front of mating sheep to insure spotted offspring. (It was believed that the offspring would look like what the mother saw during conception.) Rachel also tricked Laban by stealing the household gods (little idols or statues of gods).

Activity 13

Twelve answers are required on these variations of sociograms. A sociogram visually depicts people's relationships. Ask students to write a *feeling* or *emotion* word on each of the twelve lines drawn between characters. Discussion follows.

Activity 14

In this story, it is Jacob, rather than Laban, who perpetrates the deception. The class might consider whom they think is more morally wrong. By writing letters from Laban's point of view, they will examine the feelings of one who has been tricked.

Activity 15
Answer Key:

Abraham (Abram): selected by God to be the forebearer of a chosen race; tested by God when asked to sacrifice his own son.

Esau: firstborn of Isaac and Rebecca; favored by Isaac.

Hagar: Sarah's slave; given to Abraham as a concubine; helped by God in the Wilderness of Beersheba.

Isaac: son of Abraham and Sarah; offered as a sacrifice by Abraham; husband of Rebecca.

Ishmael: son of Abraham and Hagar.

Jacob: younger son of Isaac and Rebecca; tricked brother and father into giving him the birthright; favored by Rebecca.

Laban: Jacob's father-in-law; deceived Jacob by marrying him to Leah.

Leah: Jacob's first wife.

Lot: nephew of Abraham; asked for best land toward Sodom; saved when Sodom and Gomorrah were destroyed.

Lot's wife: turned into pillar of salt for looking back at destruction of Sodom and Gomorrah.

Rachel: Jacob's favorite wife.

Rebecca: Isaac's wife.

Sarah: (Sarai): wife of Abraham; conceived Isaac when old.

Terah: Abraham's father.

Activity 16
Answer Key:

```
V H C C A K I P A O V E B E T L N C
S L A M B O U Y V W Y X T Y E M Q A
X K U A B P K L E A N I S A R A H P
D R N S T H O I N O R I O H S T O Z
Z F F R C P D E S C E N D A N T S C
T Q E S S O T G D H W O O D L I H L
J P A N E R H Y L A M B M I B I E A
E M I J K R L P E T F A R G S T P X
I E S S N I A T E R H T E N C T H X
O F F L E D A I S E U F S L Y U E V
H O P E L G H A G A R H A N D O R W
H O H M M E T N U I C I U L S N D W
E G P N H O P G S F G O P U E B I H
N F A N L R O E C Y J H A N G E L S
I H M O L E E L D B T J H K L I S K
M I S M N K E S A F O U R T E E N Y
```

Migration Unit

Activity 1
Answer Key

1. Jacob
2. Joseph's brothers
3. Joseph's brothers
4. Joseph's brothers
5. Joseph's brothers
6. Joseph's brothers
7. Reuben
8. Joseph's brothers
9. Jacob
10. Potiphar

Activity 2

Arguments for the defense:
 Jacob's obvious favoritism toward Joseph.
 Joseph's dreams
 Reuben's attempt to save Joseph
 Any emotional appeals that a lawyer might justifiably use to sway the jury.

Activity 3

1.	O	8.	O	15.	F
2.	O	9.	F	16.	O
3.	O	10.	O	17.	O
4.	F	11.	O	18.	O
5.	F	12.	F	19.	F
6.	F	13.	F	20.	O
7.	F	14.	O		

Activity 4
The rhythm and rhyme of a limerick are best copied by reading a limerick. For those who ask for the pattern, the accented syllables(´), unaccented syllables (∪), and rhymes (underlined) have been marked below on the example.

There once was a woman, a _tease_.
Who said, "Won't you sleep with me, _please_?"
But Joseph, _appalled_,
Said, "No, not at _all_."
So she sent for the guards crying, "_Seize_!"

Activity 5
Answer Key:
clue: wine steward—execution
clue: baker—vine
clue: birthday—dreams
clue: thin cows—eight
clue: ripe grain—famine
clue: Joseph—jewels
clue: Arsenath—king's daughter
clue: dreams—grape press

Activity 6
Students are asked to perceive relationships. Under "prisoners" the suggested answers are: wine steward, chief baker, and Joseph.

Activity 7
Emotions may vary depending upon interpretation.

Activity 8
Students should draw Joseph's brothers, their donkeys, their packs, and the money that Joseph planted in their packs.

Activity 9
This is an antonym exercise. Students may expand the list of antonyms if desired. Each selected word should be explained by citing proof from the passage.

Activity 10
Examples of headlines:

Genesis 43:1-14
FATHER RISKS LIFE OF FAVORED CHILD TO SAVE FAMILY

Genesis 43:15-17
UNKNOWN VISITORS TO DINE WITH ROYAL GOVERNOR

Genesis 18—23
MYSTERIOUS MONEY FOUND IN SACKS

Genesis 43:24-34
ROYAL GOVERNOR SHOWS UNCOMMON INTEREST IN HEBREW VISITORS

Genesis 44:1-13
SILVER CUP STOLEN BY GUESTS OF GOVERNOR

Activity 11
Activity 11 draws upon the whole unit for the integration of personalities. If the teacher wishes to use only information gathered from this reading selection, the following changes should be made:
Jacob (Genesis 45:21—46:7)
Joseph (Genesis 45:1-20)
Judah (Genesis 44:18-34)
Pharaoh (Genesis 45:16-20)
Benjamin (Genesis 44:18-34)

Activity 12
Tell the students that people sending telegrams are charged per word. Therefore, most telegrams are short. This exercise emphasizes writing a clear and concise message.

Activity 13
Answer Key:
Baker: imprisoned with Joseph; beheaded by the king after Joseph's interpretation of his dream.
Benjamin: Joseph's brother; Jacob's favored son.
Jacob: Joseph's father; moved to Egypt during the famine.
Joseph: son and favorite of Jacob; intrpreter of dreams; sold by his brothers into slavery; governor of Egypt.
Judah: Joseph's half brother who advised selling Joseph into slavery instead of killing him; pledged his life for Benjamin.
King of Egypt: released Joseph from prison; dreamed about cows and stalks of grain that represented seven years of plenty and seven years of famine; placed Joseph in position of governor; gave land of Goshen to Jacob and his family.
Potiphar: king's officer; owner of Joseph; placed Joseph in prison for trying to rape his wife.
Potiphar's wife: claimed that Joseph had attempted to rape her.

Reuben: Joseph's half brother who planned to save him when the other brothers wanted to kill him; pledged the lives of his sons for Benjamin.

Simeon: Joseph's half brother who was left for ransom in Egypt.

Wine steward: imprisoned with Joseph; returned to his position in the palace after Joseph's interpretation of his dream; encouraged the king to release Joseph from prison.

Activity 14

The class is divided into groups of two after writing twenty-five questions each from the Migration to Egypt unit. Questions should not include obscure names or places.

Each player will make a token to represent him/her, placing it in the Canaan square opposite his/her opponent's square. The game begins with one player asking the other his/her top question card. If the opponent answers correctly, he/she moves ahead one square. If he/she answers incorrectly, he/she stays where he/she is. The opponent then asks player one the first question.

When all questions have been asked, the player closest to Egypt wins the game.

Wilderness Unit

Activity 1

Any of these stories could apply to the headline:
1. Fear causes the King of Egypt to place the Israelites in slavery.
2. Fear causes the Pharaoh to advise the midwives to kill the newborn baby boys.
3. Fear of God causes the midwives to disobey the king.
4. Fear causes the Pharaoh to drown the newborn Hebrew boys.
5. Fear causes the mother of Moses to place the baby in a basket on the Nile.

Counsel the students to embellish their stories with plausible details not included in the Biblical account.

Activity 2
Answer Key:

1. seventy
2. Reuben, Simeon, Levi, Judah, Issachar, Zebulum, Benjamin, Dan, Naphtali, Gad, Asher
3. Joseph
4. Israelites
5. hard labor
6. boy babies
7. three months
8. basket of reeds
9. waterproof
10. tall grass by the river
11. sister
12. king's daughter
13. Shiprah, Puah
14. Hebrew women
15. Nile
16. Pithorn, Rameses
17. supply centers
18. to bathe
19. his mother
20. slaves
21. adopted him
22. pay her
23. pull out
24. enemies
25. families
26. tar

Explanation of shape: "M" for Moses

Activity 3
Answer Key:
1. Moses saw the Egyptian kill the Hebrew man.
2. Moses killed the Egyptian the day before.
3. The king heard about Moses' action.
4. The king tried to have Moses killed.
5. Moses rescued Jethro's daughters from the shepherds.
6. God heard the cries of the Israelites.
7. Moses saw the burning bush and heard God.
8. God informed Moses that he would lead his people out of Egypt.
9. Moses asked for clarification of God's name.

Activity 4

A discussion of the questions should follow Activity 4. Do students have possible answers to the questions raised?

One suggestion is to place a student in the role of God and have the class interview him with the questions that they have formulated.

Activity 5

This activity should be completed before reading Exodus 6:28—11:10. Its purpose is to visualize the impact of the plagues on the Egyptian people.

Activity 6

The teacher might request that students include all the disasters mentioned in this selection. Tell the students to try to imagine their feelings in a similar situation. Letters may be read aloud and discussed. Then, perhaps, the students would like to invent a reply that the editor would publish in response to his mail concerning the subject of the disasters.

Activity 7

Answer Key:

11—The pillar of cloud followed the Israelites.
15—The Egyptian soldiers panicked.
3—Pharaoh told Moses to leave.
13—The sea became dry land.
1—Pharaoh's son died.
5—The Israelites started on their journey.
7—The Israelites camped at Sukkoth.
9—Pharaoh pursued the Israelites.
6—The Israelites baked unleavened bread.
10—The Israelites complained to Moses.
4—The Egyptians gave dough to the Israelites.
16—The sea covered the Egyptian army.
8—The Israelites camped at Etham.
12—Moses held his hand over the sea for the first time.
2—The Egyptians cried for the dead.
14—The Israelites walked into the sea.

Note: The Passover means to pass over or spare. This event took place when the angel passed over the Israelites' homes.

Activity 8

Answer Key:

1. Families mourn sons
2. Israelites escape with valuables
3. Egyptian army pursues Israelites
4. God parts the Red Sea
5. Army drowns in Red Sea
6. Unleavened bread result of quick move
7. Body of Joseph to be buried again
8. Pillar of fire seen in sky

Activity 9

Divide the class into groups of three. Two people will play the game; the third will be given the answer key to qualify answers and keep score.

The teacher will supply a dice or spinner for each group. The purpose of the game is to answer the most questions correctly while circling the board three times.

If a player lands on a question square, his opponent asks him/her a question about the selection. If he/she answers the question correctly, he/she receives the point. If not, the opponent receives the point.

Answer Key:

1. Elim
2. hungry
3. rain
4. ? square
5. Moses
6. quail
7. on the ground
8. two quarts
9. store any food from day to day
10. got worms in the food
11. twice as much food
12. Sabbath
13. ? square
14. gathered food
15. manna
16. Aaron
17. 40

Activity 10

Pictures could allude to the Passover, deception of the Egyptians, escape across the Red Sea, and the provisions of quail and manna.

Memento boxes may be made instead by fixing mementos of the trip to the bottom of a shoebox. Labels such as "sand from the Red Sea" would be appropriate.

Activity 11

A discussion following the activity is encouraged. Important questions to be considered are: (1) Which commandments are followed by everyone in the class? (2) Are these rules right? If so, then what makes them right? (3) Are they right for only the person who believes in them or for everyone?

Example:
You shall have no other gods before me = You shall consider me to be the only god.

Activity 12

The students will probably list some rules their parents and school make for them to follow. Emphasize that it is also important to consider commandments they set for themselves.

Activity 13

This activity should generate discussion about the characters and their values. Moses might have purchased: obedience, faith, fear of God's power. His people might choose from: a life of security, enough to eat, knowing what the future holds, more than enough to eat, protection from the Canaanites, a better leader and a guarantee of reaching Canaan.

Activity 14

The class might want to consider the root of personal and universal fears, and possible control of fears.

Activity 15

The ads written should reflect the actual desires portrayed in this section.

Activity 16

This activity is basically designed for entertainment. It suggests the difficulties of reaching Canaan.

Activity 17
Answer Key:

Aaron: Moses' brother; chosen to speak to the Egyptians; priest or Levite.

Caleb: one of twelve spies sent into Canaan; would be allowed to enter Canaan because of his advice to confront Canaanites forty years earlier.

Jethro: Moses' father-in-law; priest of Midian.

Joshua: one of the twelve spies sent into Canaan; advised Israelites to continue into the land of Canaan; Moses' successor as leader of the Israelites.

Moses: raised by Pharaoh's daughter; chosen by God to lead the Israelites out of Egypt. (Name means "to lead out.")

Zipporah: Moses' wife; Jethro's daughter.

Activity 18
Answer Key:

Promised Land Unit

Activity 1
The contracts should include all of the terms negotiated between Rahab and the spies.

Activity 2
Tell students to try to remember promotional posters from movie theaters. The posters usually try to highlight a key moment in the movie. Students should attempt the same for this selection.

Activity 3
Suggest that the class think of achievements that Joshua would be remembered for. In writing eulogies for themselves, they may consider not only their achievements to date, but also future achievements.

Activity 4
After students write titles, the teacher may ask individuals to read them aloud to see if the class members can guess which character is described.

Activity 5
Clever ads might stress comedy in the roles of Ehud, King Eglon, Deborah, Barak, or Jael.

Activity 6
Warn students to read through all of the choices before answering a question.

Answer Key:

1.	B	6.	C	11.	C
2.	A	7.	B	12.	B
3.	C	8.	C	13.	A
4.	C	9.	B	14.	C
5.	B	10.	B		

"A" answers 2   **"B"** answers 6   **"C"** answers 6

Activity 7
Answer Key:

1.	A	6.	A
2.	A	7.	A
3.	opinion	8.	opinion
4.	A	9.	A
5.	opinion	10.	A

Students may have good reasons for different answers in this exercise. Be sure to discuss opinion questions.

Activity 8
Example:
Statement 1 refers to the appearance of an angel to Manoah and his wife. Upon is appearance, they were more afraid than unafraid. The "X" on the continuum should, therefore, be closer to the word "afraid."

```
                                              X
_____
unafraid                                      afraid
```

Activity 9

Samson is surely the most unlikely candidate for a judge of Israel. To develop his character, consider Samson's pranks:
—marrying a Philistine girl
—betting thirty sets of clothes
—killing thirty Philistines for their clothes
—tying 300 foxes together
—visiting a prostitute
—escaping from Gaza

Activity 10

"Tongue in cheek" is the mood here.

Activity 11

Signposts could commemorate:
—Delilah's house (Gaza)
—prison or temple (Gaza)
—field burned by torches
—wedding place (Timnah)
—burial place of thirty Philistines (Ashkelon)
—burial place of 1,000 Philistines (Ramath Lehi)
—missing gate (Gaza)

Activity 12

Answer Key:

1.	Orpah	7.	Boaz
2.	Ruth	8.	Boaz
3.	Naomi/Ruth/Orpah	9.	Naomi
4.	Naomi	10.	Naomi
5.	Naomi/Boaz	11.	Naomi
6.	Ruth	12.	Ruth

Activity 13

Example:
Sorrow: death of one's husband when still a young woman.

Activity 14

Barak: leader of Israelite army against Sisera.
Deborah: Israelite judge who sent Barak into battle with Jabin's army.
Delilah: Samson's girlfriend who betrayed the secret of his strength to the Philistines.
Eglon: King of Moab; defeated Israel; captured Jericho; slain by Ehud.
Ehud: judge who killed King Eglon and defeated the Moabites.
Gideon: judge who defeated the Midianites.
Jabin: Canaanite king opposed by Deborah.
Jael: killed Sisera with a tent peg.
Joshua: Moses' successor as leader of the Israelites; led the tribes into Canaan.
Manoah: Samson's father.
Rahab: prostitute in Jericho who hid Israelite spies.
Samson: Nazirite; Israelite judge because he fought against the Philistines (in an *unorthodox* manner); lost his strength when he lost his hair.
Sisera: commander of Jabin's army; killed by Jael.

Activity 15

After each student has chosen sixteen names and placed them in the boxes, the teacher will arbitrarily choose descriptions and read them aloud. (Mark the ones that are used.) If a student believes that one of his names fits the description, he will place an "X" through the name. The first person to "X" four squares horizontally, vertically, or diagonally wins the game by raising their hand. (Check answers before announcing the winner.)

The game can be continued until two or three winners are found. The game can be repeated by drawing squares on other sheets of paper or by writing new descriptions for the characters.

Descriptions:
—betrayed secret of Samson's strength (Delilah)
—attacked Jericho (Joshua)
—killed Sisera (Jael)
—Samson's father (Manoah)
—only Israelite woman judge (Deborah)
—killed by a sword run through his belly (Eglon)
—tested God with sheep's fleece (Gideon)
—Philistine's god (Dagon)
—disclosed the answer to Samson's riddle (Samson's wife)
—killed with a tent peg driven through the temple (Sisera)
—accompanied Gideon to the edge of the enemy camp (Purah)
—altar dedicated to him was torn down by Gideon (Baal)
—resident of Jericho (Rahab)
—Gideon's father (Joash)
—afraid to go into battle without Deborah (Barak)
—left-handed (Ehud)
—tied 300 foxes' tails together (Samson)
—Canaanite king opposed by Deborah (Jabin)

Early Nationalism Unit

Activity 1

Instruct students to consider not only facts they have learned about Saul, but also some of his personality traits. Each spoke of the character wheel should contain one item of information.

Activity 2

Saul's speech should urge unification of the tribes of Israel, recognizing that without this the town of Jabesh would have been defeated. Unification in the future would also increase Saul's power, so it is politically expedient for Saul to show his appreciation for the prompt response to his message.

The toasts could reflect his followers' awe over: Saul's recent prophetic image, his concern for Jabesh, his leadership abilities, his magnanimous forgiveness of political enemies, or even his physical superiority.

Activity 3
Answer Key:
David: 4,8,9,5,6,10
Goliath: 1,2,3
Jonathon: 1,7,11,12
Saul: 1,2,3

Activity 4
Example:
DAVID
Always obedient son
Victorious in the name of God,
In battle, greater than Saul,
Dedicatad to Israel's cause.

Remind students to use information about Saul and David that has been given in the Biblical stories. They should *not* resort to name calling.

Activity 5
Possible scenes:
Saul throwing his spear at David.

Saul promising Merab to David but marrying her to another man.

Saul enticing David to kill a hundred Philistines in exchange for Michal's hand in marriage.

Saul ordering soldiers to bring David to him so that he can kill him.

Disguised, Saul consulting medium in order to speak with the spirit of Samuel.

Saul killing himself on the field of battle.

Activity 6
Album covers may be designed in the workbook or on larger sheets of paper. Have students include details to make their designs look like an actual record cover. Consider creating an album title and the name of the recording artists and recording company. Designs can be discussed and displayed.

Activity 7
Answer Key:
City Gate: Site of Uriah's death.
Wine: David's attempt to make Uriah drunk and go home to his wife.
Letter: David's message to Joab, plotting Uriah's death.
Mourning: Bathsheba's reaction to Uriah's death.
Lamb: Symbol of Bathsheba in Nathan's parable.

Rooftop: Location of David's observation of Bathsheba's bath.
Fasting: David's attempt to influence God when his child was ill.
Arrows: Instrument of Uriah's death.
Guilt: David's judgment of the rich man; God's judgment of David.
Death: Uriah's fate, fate of David's child.

Activity 8
This exercise is a variation on the television game, "To Tell The Truth." The students are asked to determine the "real" David from their choices of David 1, David 2, and David 3. Each David is asked the same questions. Students should circle incorrect answers. They should discover that David 2 is the *real* one.

Activity 9
Answer Key:
Factual Statements

1.	T		5.	T
2.	T		6.	F
3.	T		7.	T
4.	F			

Comprehension Statements

8.	T		10.	T
9.	T		11.	T

Synthesis Statements
Responses to synthesis may be a matter of opinion. Discuss student's responses to all statements.

Activity 10
A list of current movie stars may be placed on the board to inspire answers for the first section.

Activity 11
Answer Key:

Psalm 23	Psalm 29
shepherd	power
rest	voice
strength	seas
rod	mountains
staff	lightning
enemies	king
cup	peace
love	

Activity 12
Suggestions for Psalm 23 are:
1. lying down in green pastures
2. standing beside still water
3. walking through the Valley of the Shadow of Death
4. having the comfort of God (symbolized by his staff)
5. preparing a banquet for us

Activity 13

The purpose of this activity is to allow the class to compare the nature of their wishes to Solomon's wish.

Activity 14

The collage relates personal events and therefore need not be shared with the rest of the class.

A discussion may follow the completion of Activity 14, considering whether or not the students agree with Solomon's appraisal that the time for each of their events is chosen by God. In other words, who determines the events of one's life? (God, oneself, other people, fate, etc.)

The teacher should stress the importance of Ecclesiastes 3:1-8 as an example of Solomon's wisdom, granted to him because of his unselfish request.

Activity 15

Answer Key for Biblical completions:
Proverbs 10:7: Good people are remembered as a blessing.
Proverbs 10:12: Love forgives all.
Proverbs 10:15: Poverty destroys the poor.
Proverbs 10:20: The words of a good man are worthwhile.
Proverbs 11:29: A fool will serve the wise.
Proverbs 13:7: People who pretend to be rich often have nothing.
Proverbs 13:16: Sensible people think before they act.
Proverbs 15:1: A quiet answer soothes anger.
Proverbs 16:32: Patience is better than power.

Activity 16

Proverb illustrations may be done on sheets of construction paper. The proverbs may be taken from Activity 15. One option is to have students pass their drawings around to see if other classmates can tell what proverb is represented.

Activity 17

Students should be reminded that they are describing a modern counterpart to Job *before* he was afflicted. It is not necessary to have a particular person in mind when completing this character analysis. It might, however, be interesting to suggest the names of key figures in society who might fit this description.

Activity 18

The inscriptions on the tombstones should be descriptive. (What would each character most likely be remembered for?)

Activity 19

Answer Key:
Absalom: David's son; led a rebellion; killed while hanging from a tree.
Bathsheba: Uriah's wife; committed adultery with David; married David.

David: son of Jesse; killed Goliath; played harp for Saul; wrote many psalms; married Michal and Bathsheba; second king of Israel.
Eliphaz: Job's friend who believed that Job suffered because of his own righteousness.
Goliath: Philistine soldier over nine feet tall; challenged the Israelites.
Joab: David's military commander; complied with David's desire that Uriah be placed in a dangerous position in battle; killed Absalom.
Job: wealthy man stricken with many disasters.
Jonathon: Saul's son; David's friend.
Michal: Saul's daughter; married David.
Nathan: prophet who accused David of adultery and murder.
Samuel: anointed Saul as king.
Saul: first king of Israel; became envious of David's popularity; plotted to kill David; killed himself in battle with Philistines.
Solomon: a wise ruler; David and Bathsheba's second son; wrote Ecclesiastes; built the temple.
Uriah: Hittite convert to Judaism; married to Bathsheba; killed in battle as planned by David.

Activity 20
Answer Key:

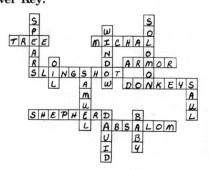

Prophetic Messages Unit

Activity 1

Suggested answers are:
1. Elijah obeyed God and hid at Cherith Brook.
2. Elijah went to Sidon.
3. The widow fed Elijah and her family for many days on few provisions.
4. Elijah brought the widow's son back to life.
5. Elijah presented himself to Ahab.
6. Elijah told Ahab that he had disobeyed God's commands by worshipping the idols of Baal.
7. Elijah asked God to send down fire for the sacrifice of the bull.
8. Elijah ordered the people to seize the prophets of Baal.

Activity 2

Encourage the class to mimic a specific sportscaster. The role of sportscaster can be assigned to a class member, and the other students can be interviewed by him.

Keep in mind:
—Elijah's confrontations with Ahab
—Ahab's worship of Baal
—Obadiah's rescue of the prophets of God
—Jezebel's persecution of God's prophets

The teacher may wish to follow this activity with an examination of the curse placed on Ahab's family, found in 1 Kings 21:1-29, 22:29-40, 2 Kings 9:14-37.

Activity 3

A thesaurus may be used for this exercise. Group work is also profitable.

A practical approach is to first list the reasons that God gave to Jeremiah for his dismay over Israel. Adjectives such as "fickle" can be adapted from the list.

The teacher may decide to assign a certain percentage of the alphabet.

Activity 4

An example of a tanka on the suggested topic is provided.
Faithful Israel—five syllables
Loved and protected by God—seven syllables
Reaped God's punishments—five syllables
Due to faithless ancestors—seven syllables
Who worshipped idols, not God—seven syllables

Group work would make this assignment less difficult.

Activity 5

Activity 5 should be completed before reading the chapter. The teacher is encouraged to discuss frustrating situations that are common to more than one member of the class.

Jeremiah 20:7-18 should be read in reference to the list. Students should watch for Jeremiah's frustrations in order to associate with his feelings in this monologue addressed to God.

Jeremiah was frustrated because he had been deceived by God, because he had been ridiculed, and because his friends had watched for his downfall.

Activity 6

Tell students to design the card and write the inside sentiment, keeping in mind appropriate drawings for the time. This can be turned into an art project by using construction paper.

Activity 7

On the disobedience half of Jonah, students might draw a ship in a storm, Jonah asleep in the ship's hold, lots being drawn to determine the guilty man, Jonah being thrown into the sea, and Jonah deep inside the fish. On the obedience half of Jonah, students might draw Jonah talking to the people of Nineveh, Jonah sitting in the shade of his shelter, and Jonah's plant.

Activity 8

Answer Key:

1.	R	9.	D	17.	H
2.	P	10.	B	18.	O
3.	I	11.	S	19.	A
4.	E	12.	G	20.	C
5.	T	13.	L	21.	B
6.	M	14.	Q	22.	J
7.	K	15.	F		
8.	N	16.	C		

(Ship bound for Tarshish, Jonah overboard)

Activity 9

Modern dialect and humorous retorts are encouraged. Less artistic students can draw stick figures, or the class can be divided into groups that combine talents of art and dialogue. Enlarged comic strips can be displayed around the room.

Activity 10

This exercise asks students to imagine how the characters would fill in the blanks. There are many correct answers. Ask students to volunteer some of their answers and discuss them.

Activity 11

Each person plays many roles in life. After the students explain how Daniel fits the nine roles listed, ask them what roles they play.

Activity 12

Keep in mind that Daniel foretold the death of Balshazzar, the enemy of Darius. Daniel also showed his power over Darius' administrators when he survived the lions' den.

Activity 13

Beyond judgment, the prophets' vision was a day of universal peace in which a messiah, or king, would rule over all nations justly.

Activity 14

Answer Key:

(+)	(−)
harvest	darkness
peace	yoke
wisdom	battle
reverence	lions
singing	fools
dance	desert
rescue	afraid
child	tired

Students should decide upon the good or bad connotations of the words based on their use in the selection. Afterwards, discuss which words seem good or bad outside of the context. Also consider words that have both good and bad connotations outside of context.

Activity 15

Abednego: Israelite exile; escaped from burning furnace.

Ahab: King of Israel; married Jezebel; built temple to Baal.

Belshazzar: King of Babylon; son of Nebuchadnezzar; lost his kingdom after seeing handwriting on palace wall.

Daniel: Israelite exiled to Babylon; read handwriting on wall for King Nebuchadnezzar; disobeyed King Darius' order and was thrown into the lions' den.

Darius: King of the Medes and Persians; invaded Babylon during Belshazzar's reign; respected Daniel.

Elijah: prophet; predicted famine in Israel; discredited and killed prophets of Baal.

Isaiah: prophet; spoke of future Kingdom of God.

Jeremiah: prophet; appointed to predict Israel's destruction; disillusioned with his role.

Jezebel: Queen of Israel; wife of Ahab; ordered death of God's prophets.

Jonah: prophet; swallowed by large fish when avoiding trip to Nineveh.

Meshach: Israelite exile; escaped from burning furnace.

Nebuchadnezzar: King of Babylon; attack Jerusalem and tool political captives.

Shadrach: Israelite exile; escaped from burning furnace.

Activity 16

Answer Key:

A = 16	J = 12	S = 24
B = 18	K = 5	T = 3
C = 7	L = 6	U = 23
D = 15	M = 19	V = 22
E = 25	N = 10	W = 1
F = 2	O = 11	X = 21
G = 26	P = 20	Y = 13
H = 14	Q = 17	Z = 9
I = 4	R = 8	

Message: The prophets did many amazing things: brought a child back to life, called down fire from Heaven, stayed alive in a fish, and survived a lion's den.

Jesus Unit

For background on Jesus' life, it is suggested that a complete gospel be read as a supplement to the selected New Testament passages in the book. A word search for the book of Mark is included for this purpose (see end of the Resources section).

Activity 1

Credit should be given in particular to students who use every letter of the word as a necessary part of the design. One method of evaluating the poems is to draw them on the blackboard and to allow the class to judge them.

The reading selection may be broadened to include an account of John the Baptist's birth (Luke 1:5-25, 1:39-80), Jesus' purification ceremony (Luke 2:21-40), the family's escape to Egypt and eventual return to Nazareth (Matthew 2:13-23), and Jesus as a boy in the temple (Luke 2:41-52).

Activity 2

Students may write "cumulative" sentences by combining two or more phrases in the context of a sentence.

Example:

In Galilee during Elizabeth's sixth month, an angel visited Mary *with a message.*

The teacher can create a game out of this activity by allowing teamwork in the preparation of cumulative sentences. The team using the most prepositional phrases in a meaningful sentence is the winner.

Activity 3

The questions should be similar to those listed below.

1. Who baptized Jesus?
2. What did John baptize with?
3. What were John's clothes made from?
4. What did the voice from heaven say when Jesus was baptized?
5. In what form did the Spirit of God appear?
6. What was John's belt made from?
7. Where did the devil taunt Jesus, suggesting that he throw himself down to be caught by angels?
8. Whom did John rail against and call snakes?
9. What did John eat?
10. How long was Jesus in the wilderness?

Activity 4

Have students read the selection and record how Jesus responded to the devil's temptations. Then, students should record temptations that they have encountered and their responses to those temptations. Class discussion may be generated from their own experiences.

Activity 5

This exercise asks students to imagine what it was like to be a disciple. They should use details in their writing.

Activity 6

Draw comparisons between those items selected by the students and those mentioned in the Bible. What important differences are there? Draw some conclusions. Then have the class consider groups that fit into the Biblical categories of those who are happy.

Below are Biblical categories:
1. the spiritually poor
2. people who mourn
3. the humble
4. people who desire to follow God's ways
5. the merciful
6. the pure in heart
7. people who work for peace
8. those who are persecuted for following God
9. Jesus' followers

Activity 7

This activity is designed to introduce the concept of a parable—a story that contains a moral or an explanation of life as it should be.

Examples:
1. The seed grows and becomes a tree, and the birds make nests in its branches.
2. The yeast causes the dough to rise.

Activity 8

A sample slogan button follows:

Father

Activity 9

Each statement is an example of one of the following ideas: (**A**) the faith Jesus had in God, (**B**) a lesson Jesus taught, (**C**) preparations made before the crucifixion, (**D**) prophecies Jesus made.

Answer Key:

1.	A	5.	D	9.	C
2.	B	6.	D	10.	D
3.	A	7.	B		
4.	D	8.	C		

Activity 10

Suggestions for sketches

Matthew 21:1-11
    Donkey
    Cloaks
    Crowd
    Branches

Matthew 21:12-17
    Overturned table
    Coins
    Pigeons

Matthew 26:17-35
    Broken bread
    Wine cup
    Table
    Thirteen people around table

Matthew 26:36-46
    Praying figure
    Three sleeping figures
    Folded hands

Matthew 26:47-56
    Sword
    Club
    Fleeing people

Activity 11

Inner conflicts should be stressed. Peter had sworn that he would never leave Jesus, yet he denied ever having known him. Judas tried to regain his innocence by returning the silver coins. Pilate sympathized with Jesus, but he was swayed by the crowd. Jesus himself asked God why he had been abandoned.

Note: Even though the Sanhedrin, the supreme Jewish council, decided to kill Jesus, they were required to send him to Pilate, the Roman administrator, for sentencing.

Activity 12

Key words are those words which express a major concept or idea in a selection. The words are listed in the order in which they occur. Some words have been taken directly from the passage; others express an idea from the selection.

Answer Key:
1. **arrest**—Jesus was arrested and taken to the house of Caiaphas.
2. **false evidence**—The chief priests tried to find false evidence against Jesus.
3. **deny**—As Jesus predicted, Peter denied him three times.
4. **rooster**—The rooster crowed after Peter denied Jesus three times.
5. **thirty silver coins**—Judas received this amount for betraying Jesus.
6. **blood money**—The silver coins were believed to be tainted, so they were used to secure land for a cemetery for foreigners.
7. **water**—Pilate "washed his hands" of Jesus and his fate.
8. **crown of thorns**—The soldiers fashioned this to mock Jesus.
9. **wine**—The soldiers offered Jesus bitter wine.
10. **clothes**—The soldiers cast lots for Jesus' clothes.
11. **temple**—The temple reflected Jesus' death when its curtain was torn in half.
12. **crucify**—Jesus was crucified.
13. **darkness**—At noon the country was covered with darkness.
14. **earthquake**—When Jesus died, the countryside was shaken by an earthquake, prompting some people to say, "He was the son of God."

Activity 13

Students are asked to imagine the reactions of various bystanders at the crucifixion. Comments might have been made about Jesus' death, religious leaders, the crowd present at the crucifixion, or Judas' disappearance and subsequent suicide.

Note: The crucifixion and resurrection accounts of the four gospels can be compared by reading: Mark 14:53—16:10; Luke 22:54—24:53; John 18:12—21:25. (Matthew was a tax collector and one of the twelve apostles. The second author, Mark, was a follower of Jesus' disciples. Luke was a physician and second generation Christian. John was an apostle and theologian.)

Activity 14

This activity encourages students to analyze the selection in terms of chronological order and main idea. After students have correctly outlined the passage, they should title their outlines.

Answer Key:
I. A Rich Man Buried Jesus
   A. Body Wrapped In Linen
   B. Body Placed In Tomb
II. Guards at Jesus' Tomb
   A. Chief Priest and Pharisees Met with Pilate
   B. Put Seal on Stone
III. Jesus' Resurrection
   A. Earthquake Rocked Area
   B. Jesus Clothed in White
   C. Guards Fearful
   D. Angel Spoke to Women
   E. Women Filled with Joy
IV. Guards Informed Chief Priests of Resurrection
   A. Priests Gave Soldiers Money
   B. Guards Implicated Disciples in Alleged Theft of Body
V. Disciples Saw Jesus
   A. Some Disciples Doubte
   B. Jesus Ordered Disciples to Find More Followers

Activity 15

This activity should be done on large sheets of construction paper. Results may be displayed.

Activity 16

As one of the most famous messages of the early Christian church, 1 Corinthians 13 proclaims that God's most important gift is love. Students are asked to find modern examples of love or concern by clipping newspaper headlines. The entire articles, or portions of them, may be designed as collages.

Activity 17

Begin by discussing the words from the activity, defining each before continuing with this activity.

Activity 18
Answer Key:
White: conqueror
Red: war
Black: famine, hunger
Pale: death (from war, hunger, disease)

Comparisons should be made between student associations and representative colors in Revelation.

Activity 19

Andrew: disciple; fisherman.

Barabbas: prisoner; chosen by crowd to be set free instead of Jesus.

Caiaphas: High Priest to whom Jesus was brought upon his arrest; claimed Jesus was guilty of blasphemy.

Gabriel: angel who visited Mary announcing Jesus' birth.

Herod: ruler of Galilee; sent kings to find Jesus' birthplace.

James: disciple; fisherman; son of Zebedee.

John: James' brother; disciple; fisherman.

John the Baptist: relative of Jesus; baptized Jesus.

Joseph: Mary's husband.

Joseph of Arimathea: prepared his own burial vault for Jesus.

Judas Iscariot: betrayed Jesus for thirty silver coins.

Mary: mother of Jesus.

Mary Magdalene: witness to the crucifixion; first person to whom Jesus appeared after his resurrection.

Peter (Simon): denied Christ three times; promised never to leave Jesus.

Pilate: Roman governor of Judea; sentenced Jesus to death while washing his hands of the responsibility.

Prodigal Son: character in parable representing erring mankind returning to God.

Activity 20

Answer Key:
1. Bethlehem
2. Parable
3. Crown of Thorns
4. Peter
5. Temple
6. John the Baptist
7. Gethsemane
8. Nazareth
9. Pilate
10. Disciples

Message: Peace on Earth